Contents

The Oxford Centre for Staff Development

6

Tutor Manual

Developing Students' Writing

*Dun Laoghaire Institute
of Art Design & Technology
School of Science & Technology*

Kate Williams
and Graham Gibbs

Published by

THE OXFORD CENTRE FOR STAFF DEVELOPMENT

Oxford Brookes University

Gipsy Lane

Headington

Oxford

OX3 0BP

Developing Students' Writing – Tutor Manual ISBN 1 873576 41 2
British Library Cataloguing-in-Publication Data. A catalogue record for
this book is available from the British Library.

Designed and Typeset in 10 on 12.5 pt Palatino and Helvetica by
Dan Barker and Thomas Nicolaou

Printed in Great Britain by
Oxonian Rewley Press Ltd
Oxford

Printed on paper produced from sustainable forests.

The strategic approach

1.1 How to use 'Developing Students' Writing'

This series consists of this Tutor Manual and five Student Guides. The guides are

1 *Essential Writing Skills* (1: EWS)

2 *Using Data* (2: UD)

3 *Scientific and Technical Writing* (3: S&T)

4 *Writing Reports* (4: WR)

5 *Writing Essays* (5: WE).

The abbreviations used in the text for cross-referencing are shown in brackets, and section references in the individual guides are shown as numbers following the title reference. For example: '5: WE, 5.6' is a reference to Student Guide 5, *Writing Essays*, Chapter 5, Section 6, 'Using other people's ideas'.

The Student Guides are designed primarily as an accessible, user-friendly resource for students working on their own on particular aspects of their writing. The material can also be used for group work, when the tutor feels that a particular activity may be of relevance to a wider group of students, or with particular groups of students with particular needs. Mature students, international students or students with alternative entry histories are examples of those who may be drawn together in this way. The activity on writing introductions on which the extract in the case study below is drawn (5: WE, 5.2) can be used to good effect with any of these groups, and with mainstream students on any course that involves essay writing. (See section 3.5O.)

The Tutor Manual

The manual is designed to provide the tutor with prompts and materials for developing the strategic framework within which the student develops specific writing skills. It takes a dual approach.

1 What **strategic action** can you take as tutor in establishing the framework within which students write? Chapter 2, 'Strategies for developing students' writing', suggests a number of specific actions and approaches, ranging from classroom strategies to institutional policies, to promote effective student writing.

2 What **supporting action** can you take as tutor to develop the specific writing skills of particular students or groups of students? Chapter 3, 'Using the Student Guides', makes close reference to the material in the guides. It suggests ways of integrating the material into a teaching programme, as well as pointers for specific referral and follow-up work. The material can be used as the basis of individual, small group, or whole group work.

Cross-references to the material and approaches in the Student Guides are made throughout the manual.

The Student Guides

The guides vary in detail to reflect the different demands of the key forms and contexts for writing, but share a common core and approach. Each starts with a chapter on 'Strategic thinking' in which the student is encouraged to

- ask key questions (to clarify the task, the purpose and context of the activity, and the processes involved in achieving it)

- look closely at the assessment criteria (guides 3–5).

The thinking behind this is that, when students engage in establishing precisely what is required and why it is required in this form, they are more likely to produce work that meets the tutor's criteria.

In each Student Guide there follows a chapter 'Glimpsing the process'. This tracks the process of producing work in the forms described in the titles: *Using Data* (2), *Scientific and Technical Writing* (3), *Writing Reports* (4) and *Writing Essays* (5). It gives practical step-by-step guidance to the processes often invisible to the tutor marking the finished product, but which dominate the student's life for the duration of the cycle of a particular assignment.

The remaining chapters in guides 3–5, 'Writing the . . . ' (report, essay), give detailed step-by-step advice on how to write in the required forms, based on numerous models and activities in which the student has the opportunity to practise specific sub-sets of skills. All the guides consider throughout the text a range of styles and conventions for writing within each broad category. Guides 4 and 5 end with an outline of how to approach tasks increasingly set by tutors as alternatives to the traditional forms of academic writing.

Student Guides 1 and 2 share many characteristics with the others, but have key differences that enable them to be used in different ways.

Student Guide 1, *Essential Writing Skills*, is designed as a course companion in an open learning format for students working on specific aspects of foundation writing skills, with a focus on sentence and paragraph structure. Some activities are also suitable for group work, and full explanations and comments are given as guidance for students working on their own.

Student Guide 2, *Using Data*, includes three substantial workshops on different topics (health promotion, education and social policy) as the context for developing skills in data presentation and interpretation, and the selective use of data as evidence in discussion and debate. While the text contains full answers and feedback to support students working on their own, the material lends itself to group work in subjects where confidence in data interpretation is fundamental to the course.

1.2   The dual approach to developing writing skills

The approach to developing students' writing taken in this series, as has already been mentioned, is a dual one: to consider what strategic action the tutor can initiate to promote good writing; and to develop ways of responding to specific problems as they occur.

Strategic action

This approach involves asking key questions:

Why am I setting this writing task? What is this particular task designed to achieve?

Who is it for? What audience should the student writer be addressing? What actual audience – self, tutor, other students? What hypothetical audience – assignment scenario? What are the implications of the audience for the form and style of the student's writing?

What exactly do you want your students to produce? What are the specific characteristics of a good piece of writing in this form?

Your answers to these questions will determine the nature of the task you set, and form the basis of the assessment criteria by which you will judge students' work. Specific strategies to try are outlined in Chapter 2.

It is also worth thinking through the processes the students will engage in as they work towards achieving the task.

How should they tackle each stage of the preparation and drafting involved in the task?

When should each stage be completed by, to ensure deadlines are met with the minimum of last-minute cobbling together?

Where should the various elements of the research and preparation take place? On what resources should students draw?

Your answers to these questions will determine the nature and detail of the guidelines you give to students on how to carry out a sensible and thorough programme of work, within the constraints of time, people available, equipment and so on.

These key questions form the basis of Chapter 2 ('Strategic thinking') in the Student Guides. Each guide also considers the processes involved in the various writing forms from the student's perspective.

Supporting action

This will be specific to the strengths and weaknesses shown by individual students and groups of students in each batch of written assignments. Obviously, in building preparatory work into the process of setting assignments, tutors draw on their experience of how previous groups of students fared in completing similar tasks.

The case study which follows considers how this dual approach might be drawn on in thinking about the next steps in developing the writing skills of one particular student.

1.3   What's the problem? A case study

As tutors, our primary point of contact with student writing is when we are faced with a pile of essays or assignments for marking and assessment. Each essay is something of a moment of reckoning, not only for the student, but also for the tutor: what is the quality of this student's learning in evidence in this piece of work? What progress has the student made? What skills has she or he developed? When you assess a student's work you form a view on these matters, and then have to find a way of conveying your view (or assessment) to the student.

Run through the process again: how do you react to the piece of student writing below? It is the first paragraph of an essay in response to the question

```
What are the reasons for staffing problems within the hotel
and catering industry? Suggest ways in which these might be
overcome.
```

As is the case with all industries the Hotel and Catering Industry is a great contributer to Gross National Product. Being in the top five industries means that it contributes higher than average amounts. Unlike most industries Hotel and Catering relies heavily upon Tourism from abroad. So even if there is a recession in a particular country there will still be a certain amount of income, through visitors from abroad. As travel become both cheaper and easier tourists will come from further afield, so will increase overall. In 1989, the year that the British Tourist Authority was established there were 5 million overseas visitors, to Britain. By 1992 this figure had risen to 18.5 million. By the end of 1993 it is forecast that foreign visitors will have spent £24 billion in the UK, thus helping pay foreign debt payments, but also increasing foreign currency reserves.

Your response? Your first reaction may be one of despair, or even irritation, as you chart the catalogue of deficiencies in this piece of writing.

- It does not answer the question. This student does not seem to have noticed that there is a question – *reasons* for staffing problems and *suggestions* for overcoming them – let alone tried to answer it. Instead there is mass of completely irrelevant information – *GNP, tourism, £27 billion.*

- There is no structure to the paragraph – no notion of a paragraph developing a single idea.

- The writer has done some reading and come up with some 'facts' – all unreferenced and untraceable (as well as irrelevant).

- The writer makes assertions without supporting evidence. (*As travel become both cheaper and easier tourists will come from further afield, so will increase overall.*)

- The student's use of the conventions of grammar and spelling is uncertain: use of capitals (*'Tourism'* is one of several); commas (with clauses); confusion of words (*'pay of'* for *'pay off'*); agreement of verbs (*'travel become'* for *'becomes'*); spelling (*'currancy'* for *'currency'*).

Both tutors and students know that on the basis of a particular piece of writing, the quality of the student's learning in the subject will be assessed – and in the case of this student, found seriously wanting. In brief, little credit can be given for any knowledge about the subject the individual has gained because the skills with which it is articulated are so poor. Until this student learns the conventions of academic writing, she or he cannot look forward to academic success.

Then comes the tricky bit. The tutor marking this piece of work has to find a way of giving the student feedback on their essay. At this moment, are you a judge or a teacher? Are you commenting retrospectively on the product or are you aiming to change the student's writing behaviour? Are you there to give a summative assessment or are you able to give formative feedback?

In practical terms, you have a number of options:

- give a mark, and a brief comment justifying it

- point out the errors in greater or lesser detail in the hope that the student will see what they are, and avoid them next time

- try and engage the student in understanding the purpose behind the forms and conventions of academic writing – to motivate them to put in the effort required to develop the necessary writing skills.

You will, of course, adopt all three approaches to assessment and feedback at different points in the academic cycle, but the last is the approach around which this series has been developed.

To return to this particular essay . . .

The context

The essay was set as one element of the assessed coursework in a Hotel and Catering Management module which includes a wide range of forms for student writing and learning. The module is assessed 60 per cent by examination and 40 per cent by coursework. The coursework has three elements.

1 **Workshop** (10%)   Groups of two or three students are given a topic, together with suggested reading and ideas for research. They are also given three learning outcomes which state what each workshop member should be able to do by the end of the session. The documentation required includes a handout for workshop members. An example of this is given in Section 3.4H.

2 **Individual portfolio** (15%) This is for students to collect and record evidence of their own learning, and their reflections on these experiences in relation to the concepts and ideas that underpin the module. Detailed and structured guidelines are given. (An extract from the course handbook and from a student's portfolio is given in section 3.5V.)

3 **Essay** (15%) A title is set, criteria for assessment are given, and guidance is offered on length (1500 words).

The activity

1 Strategic thinking

Put yourself in the position of the tutors who drew up this module. Consider each of the three forms of writing required for the coursework in relation to the key questions outlined above.

Record your comments in grid form.

	Why?	**Who?**	**What?**
Workshop			
Individual portfolio			
Essay			

The department concerned has evidently taken the view that clearly differentiated tasks will prompt effective learning and writing. The essay is only one of several forms of writing, and has a purpose distinct from the other forms of writing set. That said, this student writer shows a poor grasp of the skills that underpin essay writing. What do you do about it?

2 Supporting action

Are there other students in the group who share a similar lack of experience of the essay form and style? If so, it may be worth doing a whole group activity (see section 2.11) on one or more of these key aspects of essay writing.

Examples of follow-up group work

Work on	Suggested material
• analysing the question	5: WE, 3.1, 3.2
• planning an answer	5: WE, 3.3
• types of question and styles of answer	5: WE, 3.4–3.8
• developing judgement	
• writing introductions and conclusions	5: WE, 5.2, 5.7

Can you establish links between students to promote peer activity and feedback (see section 2.8 below)? Many of the weaknesses in the piece of writing in the case study would have been picked up in a simple peer feedback exercise: complete failure to address the question, unreferenced facts and errors in accuracy were all spotted quickly by students working on this material. The material could be used for a set out-of-class activity, with a brief report-back at a later session.

Are the weaknesses shown in this piece of writing specific to the particular student? Examples of the additional specific references the tutor might make for this student are shown below.

Examples of follow-up individual work

The weaknesses include the following.

Problem	Follow-up needed	Suggested material
Unstructured paragraph	How to write paragraphs	1: EWS, 7 5: WE, 5.3
Unreferenced 'facts'	Conventions of referencing – how and why	5: WE, 5.6 1: EWS, 9
Unsupported assertion	Use of evidence in argument	5: WE, 5.5 1: EWS, 9
Poor grammar, punctuation	Drafting, redrafting and proof reading	5: WE, 4.4–4.8 1: EWS, passim
Spelling		1: EWS, 8
	Spelling strategies – not relevant here; errors likely to be a result of lack of checking, and a lack of conviction of the need to check.	

Beyond this, the student needs to develop the ability to judge the effectiveness of their own writing. It may be helpful to use a a self-assessment checklist (see section 2.8) in the next piece of writing they undertake.

1.4   Writing as a learning process

The assumption that underlies this series of Student Guides is that it is helpful to see writing as a process. While the process results in a product that readers rightly expect to conform to certain norms – with a certain appearance, length and language, and an arrangement of material with a beginning, a middle and an end – the process by which it is produced is far from linear. The stages involved are outlined in the chapters 'Glimpsing the process'. These stages are not necessarily sequential; we know from our own experiences as writers that we criss-cross between the stages of the process, planning, drafting, adding, checking as we work towards a form we feel our readers will find accessible and persuasive.

However, although writing may feel chaotic at the time, with hindsight a process with some sequence in time and phasing is discernible. Tutors draw on this experience in steering students through it. In the guides, students are asked to reflect on the processes they go through in producing a piece of written work, and to link it with a particular learning cycle:

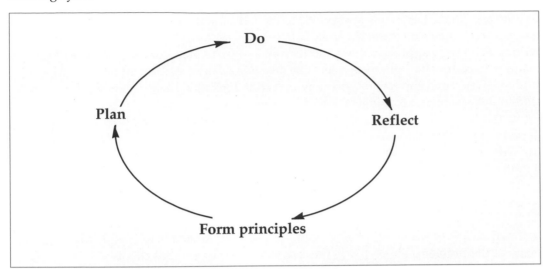

This learning cycle is used explicitly in the Student Guides to show the link between the learning process and the process of writing: see 3: S&T, 6; 4: WR, 1.7, 5.1 and 5.2; 5 WE, 6.1.

Less easy to see and direct is the nature and impact of the tutor's feedback as part of the process in prompting reflection and forming principles ready for the next time around – the second leg of the communication process. From the student's point of view, this is focused on the tutor's reaction to their writing. How successful was it? Did it meet the reader's expectations, or did it place obstacles in the reader's way by failing to exploit or observe the conventions? The anxiety generated by such concerns – not that students would express them in this way – is all the more acute when the reader is audience, judge and jury.

This second leg is a tricky one for tutors, and focuses attention on the nature, purpose and quality of feedback. Running in parallel through this pack of materials is a commitment to engage students in active ways of learning to understand the purpose and nature of writing conventions: for example, getting students to figure out what criteria their work will or should be assessed by; seeing why 'faults' are irritants to the reader; putting themselves in the place of their reader in assessing the work of others; deciding how much basic information to put across and how much can be assumed as shared. Ways of doing this are outlined in the next chapter, and can be thought of as 'interactive feedback'.

In short, the aim of the Student Guides is to talk students through their part of the writing process: from analysing and understanding the task, through the processes involved in researching and writing the piece, to a brief consideration of how to respond to feedback. The aim of the Tutor Manual is to highlight the strategic actions tutors can take in establishing the framework within which the student writes: the context of the task, setting the specific task, and giving feedback and initiating activities to develop particular skills seen to be lacking in the written product the first time around.

Strategies for developing students' writing

The case study in the previous chapter illustrates the way in which problems with writing are interlinked. Some are specific to the individual, others are shared by a wider group, others may stem from the task itself. For this reason, problems with student writing need to be approached in a number of ways – divided, for the purposes of this manual, into strategic initiatives tutors can take in establishing the context in which students write, and supporting or follow-up action for individual students and groups of students. This chapter considers strategic actions, ranging from strategies individual tutors can introduce within their courses to those that need wider support within the department or institution as a whole. Chapter 3 suggests specific supporting action for use with individual students and groups, drawing on the materials and approaches in the Student Guides.

2.1   What's the problem (2)?

In the overview of student problems with writing summarized below, you will recognize many of the problems illustrated in the case study in the previous chapter.

Problems with writing

- Misunderstanding the question or answering the wrong question

- Misunderstanding the topic, having a confused overview of the topic or simply lacking knowledge

- Misunderstanding the form of writing expected (What is an 'essay'? A 'report'?)

- Having an inappropriate audience in mind, or ignoring the needs of the audience

- Lack of basic writing competence: grammar, spelling, sentences and paragraph construction

- Lack of knowledge of the writing conventions used in the discipline (use of headings, referencing, language, for example)

It is not always easy to distinguish between these problems. Poor paragraph construction, for example, may be caused by a lack of understanding of the subject rather than by a lack of ability to write paragraphs – although the reverse is more often the case. Many students need to be taught the skills of developing a single thought into a paragraph: explaining, illustrating, commenting in a way that satisfies the reader. It is also true that the quality of the writing of an individual student may vary depending on nature of the task they face. In approaching problems with student writing by means of the dual strategy outlined above, the chances of making a useful diagnosis of the problem and taking the first steps towards a positive response to it are greatly increased.

2.2 Clarifying writing tasks

Do the students understand the kind of writing task they have been set? Do they understand the differences between the major forms, and the range of styles within each form. For example:

Tutor instruction	Student options
Write me a	
Lab report	What are the sections?
	Informal notes or formal lab report?
	Personal or impersonal style?
	What are the specific conventions in the subject?
Report	Who is the reader? Real? Hypothetical?
	What goes where? What goes in the body? What in the appendix?
	What are the major headings?
	Do I use numbering systems?
Essay	How is this different to a report?
	Do I use headings or continuous prose?
	What style is right? Factual? Or is a judgement required?
	Is personal experience and comment required or penalized?

These differences matter to the student whose knowledge or experience of the conventions of the subject cannot be taken for granted. There are marked differences between the style of writing expected in different disciplines: what a historian would consider terse, a biologist might consider waffly. The use of headings is encouraged in, say, geography, but would be unacceptable in English. Students may be required to imitate professional forms of writing (as in law or business subjects) or develop a discursive style particular to the academic context.

Tutors also need to be aware that these differences in the form and style of writing expected of students exist not only between disciplines but also between individual tutors within the same discipline or groups of disciplines. This will particularly affect students working in interdisciplinary fields. Students training for the healthcare professions, for example, will need to produce work that satisfies the requirements and priorities of the tutors in more than one subject discipline – for example, science (short, highly structured lab reports, accurate notation of quantities) and clinical nursing (meticulous referencing of professional interpretations); and also on occasion to write in a more personal and reflective style. They need explicit guidance on each form.

Below are three approaches used by tutors to communicate to students what is required of them in writing an essay.

Specifying what each grade means

This exercise can be used to help students see the standards, values and criteria on which you draw when you mark their work. It clarifies what is expected of an answer which would gain different grades and, doing so, clarifies the nature of the writing task students are undertaking. It does not spoonfeed students clues about content, but provides them with a tool to help them recognize what they are doing in their writing, and what messages they are giving their reader.

You could link this with a group activity in analysing the question, based on the specific analytical approach adopted in 5, WE, 3 (see Section 3.5D below). Following this method, the essay question below would look like this:

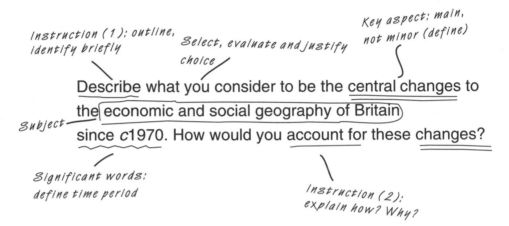

First class

Identify the central changes to the economic and social geography of Britain since *c*1970, considering carefully what is meant by these words, and pinpointing the time period you are describing. Demonstrate the link between the changes you identify as 'central' (factors or processes) and social and economic change, and explain why these processes occurred. Throughout the essay, use specific empirical evidence, referenced to your sources, to support points in your argument. You will have gone beyond the basic reading list in your research, and your answer will show that you understand the controversies in the literature that describes and explains these changes. Your essay will show a structure and logic throughout: your paragraphs show clear development of each point; your conclusion links back to the issues indicated in the introduction and shows your reader that you have formed a view about the merits or complexity of the different interpretations.

Upper second class

Describe the central changes to the economic and social geography of Britain since *c*1970, focusing on the key aspect (*central changes*) and the stated scope of the subject (*economic and social geography*) in Britain since that time. You will use accurately referenced empirical detail from the literature to support points in your argument. You may make reference to the controversies in the literature on the nature or causes of the changes, but you will not evaluate them or develop a clear viewpoint of your own. You will use only material covered in class and from the compulsory reading list. Your essay will have a clear beginning, middle and end, and well developed paragraphs. In your conclusion you will show how you have covered what you set out to do.

Lower second class

Describe some of the recent changes to the human geography of Britain. Do not be too precise in identifying the changes or in giving evidence to support your argument. Loosely relate those changes to some of the factors or processes that may have caused them, without going too far into the reasons for apparent change. Do not recognize the complexity of what has occurred or the uncertainty of interpretation. Stick closely to the material given to you in class and some of the compulsory reading. Do not show how different thinkers and writers interpret the evidence or advance a clear argument of your own. Your essay may start out with a promising introduction, but is less likely to have a satisfactory conclusion, and some of your points will be hard to find in the body of the essay.

Third class

Write an 'all-I-know-about' essay on the recent changes to the geography of Britain. Make vague and unsubstantiated statements about the changes. Throw in now and then some comments about these changes being the result of factors or processes but don't show the links between them. Give very little evidence for your assertions and restrict that evidence to what you learnt in class and some of the compulsory reading. Either construct a simple argument that has little or no logic or supporting evidence or throw in a variety of conflicting and poorly thought out ideas . . . This lack of consistency will show in the appearance of your essay. Paragraphs are likely to be too long, too short, or both, giving your reader the visual clue that you are rambling. While you may have some sort of this-is-what-I'm-going-to-say introduction, it is highly unlikely that you will have a meaningful conclusion.

Fail

Write down almost anything you can think of about Britain's geography but don't attempt to structure it in any way. Jump about between the changes and the causes, so your reader can't see the difference between them – which tells them that you can't see the difference anyway. Make unsupported statements and, where any evidence is offered, stick to what you vaguely remember from one or two of the classes you attended. Leave the reader wondering if you have learnt anything from the course. . .

Talking students through the process

A history tutor gives detailed guidance to pairs of students, in brief ten-minute slots, before they write an essay:

> I always set essays in the form of a question. Your task is to write an argument to convince your reader of your best understanding of the issues. The reader is absolutely not me, the tutor . . . it's a fellow student who happens not to have chosen that essay question. Imagine this student saying to you, 'Tell me about it.' What you put in and what you leave out depends on your link with your reader – you know your reader, and what they know and understand. You've got to convince them of your interpretation . . . this will inform your judgement about basics such as structure and length . . . but if your essay is too short, you are unlikely to have developed the argument fully enough.
>
> You've got to have a structure: a beginning, a middle and an end. You've got to be especially aware of your reader in your introduction. Give your reader an outline of your arguments, methods, problems and approaches, so they are aware of what's ahead . . . The middle, this is the bulk of your essay. This is where you make your case, using evidence, your critical reading of other historians. You've got to acknowledge sources and reference every quote – this is how you link your argument to the evidence.
>
> In your conclusion, you're saying, 'I've done it, dear reader. You've seen my case, my arguments and my evidence. Let me just point out the main thing I want you to take away from this . . .', and look outward to make links with other events, parallel situations, perhaps at a different time, or different place . . .

Written guidelines

Many tutors give students written criteria by which their work will be assessed. This can double as advice on the form and style of the writing task. For examples of written assessment criteria, see Section 2.4 below and the references to the Student Guides.

2.3   Changing writing tasks

Why am I setting this task?

Who is it for?

What exactly do I want the students to produce?

One outcome of asking yourself these strategic questions may be to think about extending the range of writing tasks you ask students to undertake. This route led the tutors of the Hotel and Catering Management module outlined in the case study in Section 1.3 to develop the present range of writing tasks. Equally, it may serve to underline the purpose of existing writing tasks. Students taking the Basic Physics module (described in 3: S&T, 2.2) are told why they have to write lab reports:

> Success in the professions and in management depends on the ability to explain to others the events, processes, plans and problems which are dealt with day by day. Writing lab reports is excellent training for such responsibilities.

What matters is that the form in which students are asked to write has a purpose to which they can subscribe.

Below are listed (in the left-hand column) a number of tasks students are frequently set, with alternatives suggested in the right-hand column. The essential point about these alternative tasks is that they should have a sense of 'real audience' for whom the piece of work is being written or delivered, and, linked to that, a sense of 'real purpose'.

Advice to students about writing in these alternative forms is given in 4: WR, 5, and 5: WE, 6.

Tasks often set	Alternatives . . .
Short answer question	Devise an encyclopaedia entry
Terms and definitions*	Produce an A–Z of . . .
Survey and statistics question	Write an answer to a client's question
Technical report*	Tender for a contract
Lab report*	Field log*
	Scientific paper
	Instructions for other students/users
Project report	Prepare a committee of inquiry report
	Document a planning application hearing
	Impact assessment of . . . (e.g., legislation)
	Draw up a consultancy brief
	Carry out a consultancy brief

Seminar paper	Documentation and presentation for a 'Court of Enquiry' (over several weeks)
	Workshop* to deliver specified learning outcomes
Report*	Report in role* (e.g., on consultancy exercise, including costings of time)
	Minutes (of meeting/simulation)*
	Presentation + handout*
Essay*	Reflective diary*
	Portfolio*
	300-word essay*
	Article*
	Poster*
	Writing in the style of . . . - learning materials for younger pupils/students - a draft answer to a parliamentary question - a letter in response to . . . - a formal speech - a pamphlet*

*These forms are considered in the series.

2.4   Specifying assessment criteria

Specifying criteria can be helpful to students in a number of ways.

- It shows the students what they will be assessed on, which goes some way towards reducing the sense of arbitrariness experienced by students who do not understand the form required.

- It gives the student specific guidance on the characteristics of the writing required before and while they are writing.

- It is helpful as a basis for self- and peer assessment before the tutor marks the work (see Section 2.8 below). If the students use this feedback, the work eventually handed in for marking and assessment is likely to be of a higher quality.

There are examples of assessment criteria, expressed in a variety of ways and in different subjects, throughout this series.

1 Psychology practical report (3: S&T, 2.2)

The extract from the checklist of comments on a psychology practical report makes clear to students the detailed technical expectations of this highly specific type of report writing.

2 Business studies report (4: WR, 2.2)

This short extract is an example of how assessment criteria can be used to provide students with a virtual outline of their reports, giving implicit guidance about the value and length of each section.

3 Construction engineering technical report (4: WR, 2.2)

The activity here asks students to draw up their own assessment criteria for the task outlined. The answer section shows the tutor's assessment criteria, on which students are also asked to assess their reports before they hand them in.

4 Geology essay (5: WE, 2.2)

This example of criteria and guidance is an illustration of an informal handwritten format which gives effective feedback to this tutor's students.

5 Planning essay (5: WE, 2.2)

This completed sheet shows how the tutor has combined the criteria, the rating scale and the comments on one sheet, and applies the criteria to a particular piece of writing.

6 Psychology essay (5: WE, 2.2)

This feedback sheet (4 x A4 sides in the original) is an example of extremely detailed assessment criteria. The front sheet provides a summary of the criteria, which are unpacked and specified in the sub-sections of the subsequent sheets. These sub-sets could be used as in (7) below.

7 English and drama

The following set of assessment criteria was used to attune students to the qualities expected of essays on a course in English literature and drama. By working on each section of the criteria in turn within class sessions, students gained an understanding of each sub-set of skills of this form of writing. Eventually the full set was used as assessment criteria.

Essay Marking Criteria					
Knowledge					
Text	deep, thorough, detailed	...	...		superficial
Author	wide knowledge used in analysis	...	...	...	no knowledge or not used
Genre	wide knowledge used in analysis	...	...	...	no knowledge or not used
Historical and social context	wide knowledge used in analysis	...	...	...	no knowledge or not used
Essay					
Structure	clear, logical structure	...	...	...	confused list
Quotations	correct, purposeful use properly referenced	...	...	...	incorrect, arbitrary use
Other sources	wide range, relevant properly referenced	...	...	...	few, irrelevant improperly referenced
Grammar, spelling	correct ...	...	...	...	...	many errors

Personal

Response to text	vivid, personal	...	...	...	little response
Viewpoint	clearly expressed		...	...	...	no viewpoint
Creativity	imaginative, surprising	...	...	...	predictable

Critical Theory

Understanding	clear grasp	...	...	...	...	little grasp
Use of methods	wide range appropriate use	...	...	...	...	little or inappropriate use

8 Education dissertation

Below is a further example of criteria, this time for a dissertation.

Dissertation Criteria

a) Clear statement of the focus/area/topic/problem/hypothesis.

b) Substantive review of the relevant literature. Good relation of theory and literature to the actual research undertaken, including justification of research topic/programme/setting(s).

c) Choice of appropriate research method(s).

d) Clear description of the research method(s), setting(s) and programme.

e) Appropriate and sufficient collection and clear presentation of data.

f) Thoroughness of critical analysis and evaluation of the research, with clear and detailed reference to data and to literature, appropriate theories and explanations and some appraisal of validity and value.

g) Sensitivity to problems and processes of research undertaken, e.g., ethics, communication, negotiation, collaboration, dissemination.

h) Substantial conclusion raising key issues and points, with suggestions for future research/practice as appropriate.

i) Full, accurate bibliography. Appendices as appropriate.

An activity on getting students to generate criteria is set in 5: WE, 2.2.

2.5   Providing models

One of the most effective ways of training anyone in a skill is to provide models for them to consider and discuss. This is equally true of developing writing skills. You can provide students with models in a number of ways.

1 Refer students to the library

As part of their preparation and research, ask students to look up

- particular articles you have identified as good models of specific forms of writing (e.g., book reviews, articles in academic journals)

- dissertations of past students – again selecting ones that are good models.

2 Circulate excellent pieces of work

To get students to identify the precise characteristics of a piece of good writing, ask them to complete an assessment sheet based on one of the more detailed models above (Section 2.4, example 1, 6 or 7).

Models of good writing are as helpful for established formats, such as lab reports, as for less well established formats, such as individual portfolios. Where you are introducing a new form, such as portfolios, and are looking for models, you might think about contacting colleagues in another institution where that form has been current for longer.

3 Annotate a good example

Detailed annotations on a piece of work, showing how a student has successfully incorporated particular features into their writing (or not), can give useful 'How to . . .' guidance to others. An example of this is given in 3: S&T, 3.5. Again, it can be useful to show specifically how the piece has met the assessment criteria.

4 Run a marking exercise

Marking exercises help students to identify the characteristics of successful and unsuccessful writing, and to discriminate between them. This is an effective way of cultivating students' judgement as a basis for developing their own writing skills.

For how to run an exercise of this sort, see section 3.5O below.

Mark two or three essays

Your choice of essays will depend on what you want to draw out. If you include an excellent essay, you have a perfect model, but students may write it off as unattainable (or a fake!). A fairly good example and one which is just below average will encourage discrimination, and prompt comments on how to make the good one better. You may simply want to show a range of acceptable or good ways of tackling the problem, in which case you will choose reasonably good pieces that illustrate different approaches.

Mark sections of several essays

There are advantages to exposing students to several examples of other students' writing. However, you cannot do this effectively within a session with complete pieces of work (unless they are very short) because you would simply have too much material to photocopy and read, and too broad a focus. Exercises based on half a dozen short examples of the same thing are good for developing students' judgement and ensure the focus is on a specific part of the whole piece. The discussion section of a technical report, the abstract of a longer lab report or introductions and conclusions of an essay work well used in this way. Examples of these last as ready-to-roll activities are given in 5: WE, 5.2 and 5.7 respectively.

These exercises are easy to put together yourself. As long as you have six or more examples of a cross-section of student writing, most of the characteristics you want to discuss will arise spontaneously from the material. Keep the examples in the original form, handwritten or word processed, to generate comment about the appearance of work!

2.6   Giving feedback on writing

Like anyone else, students need feedback on their work to know what they have done well and what they need to improve. Many examples of the forms in which feedback can be given can be found in this chapter (see Section 2.4 above) and elsewhere in the pack. This section is confined to a few strategic thoughts.

Run through the process again: how do you react to this feedback?

Some good points have been made, and the fact that your essay is not always analytical, but gives numerous examples of . . ., entirely conveys the gap existing between the . . . and the weakness of academic developments on that particular subject.

Your essay tends to be rather repetitive and your argument circular. The distinction between . . . and . . . is implicit to your main argument, but not clearly exposed. Further, although you often stress the variety of . . . and definitions of . . ., you do not really try to clarify and develop this point. On the one hand, you could have shown the . . . On the other hand . . .

This is useful analytical comment, but consider the context: this was written on an end-of-year exam paper. The tutor must have forgotten that there was no student on the receiving end and was, in effect, musing aloud – another question of audience. After marking, the papers will be sent to the examinations department for archive purposes until they are eventually shredded! All the tutor needed to do was to write '58%', or whatever.

This example may seem extraordinary, but it is not. Tutors put a lot of time and effort into detailed and thoughtful comments on students' work, but what happens next? Do students collect the work? Often they do not, especially when the piece is at the end of the module/year/course and the student's only interest lies in the grade. Do students read the comments? It appears that often they do not. Do students act on the comments? Sometimes, but more often not. These unwelcome thoughts should prompt tutors to think about the context in which they give and students receive feedback.

Why are you giving feedback?

Is it designed to be formative (early or mid-course/module) or summative (end of course/module)? The nature of the feedback you give depends on why you are giving it: if the purpose is formative, you are aiming to give feedback in such a way that it results in changed behaviour in terms of writing skills. This will be to

- encourage the student to repeat examples of the best bits and best features of their writing
- to get students to re-read their work and reflect on it.

These objectives will lead you to think about ways of engaging students in the processes involved in writing, and the reasons why they should follow up the suggestions you make. If your purpose is summative, the aim of your comments is more likely to be to explain or justify a mark or grade.

In practical terms, comments made with a summative purpose are likely to be confined to identifying faults and (hopefully) triumphs. Comments made with a formative purpose are more likely to translate this identification of faults into a hit list of specific remedial actions. The analysis of faults in the piece of student writing in Section 1.3 above shows this process in action: one fault was the use of unreferenced facts; the suggested remedial action is to engage the student in an understanding of **why** it is important to reference, and to show them, or direct them to a source that shows them, **how** to do it. This is the approach taken in 1: EWS, 9.

How detailed should feedback be?

This is an individual matter, but there is a strong argument for giving more detailed and specific feedback earlier in the course (see Section 2.4 above, examples 1, 6 and 7). The amount of feedback appropriate towards the end of the course will vary from one context to another: will the students need these skills or this knowledge as a foundation for the next stage of their studies? If you are looking at writing as a transferable skill that you have a part in helping students to develop over a three-year period, there is every reason to continue to highlight aspects of writing skills they need to work on (see Section 2.13 below). Detailed comments about the subject, however, may be irrelevant at the end of the degree/year/module, in which case you may decide to confine yourself to comments that explain the grade you have awarded – again, a question of being attuned to the needs, interests and motivation of your audience.

What form should feedback be in?

Again, this is an individual matter – between two parties, the tutor and the student. What matters is that the chosen method is an effective form of communication, and that the student's responses is active – geared towards understanding what the tutor is driving at, and effecting change.

Engaging students in the processes of learning saves academic time spent in constant repetition of the same points to different students in the group – or the same point to the same student who does not understand why a feature of their writing is unsatisfactory.

2.7   Giving feedback on process

4: WR, 3.8, anticipates initiatives by tutors to assess the process by which a piece of work is produced. The possibilities outlined are the need to:

- demonstrate the validity of early researches (by submitting an outline of research processes, or of the content of a report or dissertation)

- show the effectiveness of team work (by presenting a group plan)

- show the extent of outside contacts (by talking through a contact network)

- write an account of the group dynamics (how the group got on, allocated tasks, etc. The bridge report (3: S&T, 3.8; 4: WR, 4.6) shows this in action

- submit the report in two parts: basic research first, discussion/conclusions and recommendations later (see 4: WR, 2.1).

The strategy of using peer feedback (see Section 2.8 below) is another way of intervening in the process of writing to improve the quality of the final product the tutor has to mark.

2.8   Using peer feedback and self-assessment

It is always useful to have an outsider's view of one's work; at some point, everyone gets too close to what they are doing to make reliable judgements about the quality of their output. It can be as destructive for students to have an unduly pessimistic view of their work as it is to have an unduly optimistic one – neither promotes good work or good writing. (This is touched on in 5: WE, 4.1.) Nevertheless, it is hard for most people to expose themselves to criticism where they feel most vulnerable, and so students may well not take advice to talk through their plans with or show an early draft to someone else.

It can be helpful to promote students' confidence in the value of an external eye to build peer assessment into the course as a structured activity.

Using peer feedback

When the students have written a first draft of a piece of work, pair them up to read each other's efforts and ask them to give each other detailed feedback. The second draft, to be handed in to the tutor for marking, is accompanied by an account of how each student used the feedback: 'I've included more sources because the first draft was criticized for relying too heavily on just two.' 'I've kept the introduction exactly the same even though it was said to be unclear because I don't agree . . .'

This approach is helpful in a number of ways:

- it develops students' critical faculties on a genuine piece of work before formal assessment

- significantly better work is produced

- it is more like the 'real world', in which good writing involves redrafting in the light of criticism

- where this two-stage process takes the place of a second piece of work, the marking load for the tutor has been reduced.

(Brown et al. (1994), from which this approach is drawn, suggest a number of ways of using peer assessment to develop students' judgement in writing skills.)

Using self-assessment

By the time students reach university, they have probably been through ten years of education during which their teachers have told them to check their work before they hand it in. The student whose work appears on page 7 of this guide is one of the many who still do not. Explicit self-assessment is a way of encouraging students to reflect on their work and to see it from their reader's perspective. It also helps to elevate the process so students see it as an essential part of the extensive drafting and redrafting that underlies polished writing. Below are some suggestions for building self-assessment into the writing process.

- **A simple statement** such as 'Read, checked and corrected' (signed) . . .; or a comment on how a particular feature was arrived at – e.g., the introduction or conclusion.

- **A simple checklist** of specific points to look for. This could be

  – a sub-set of skills as a focus for this particular piece (see Section 2.4, examples 1, 6 and 7)

  – a requirement to identify and mark the parts of the structure of the essay (along the lines of the sketch 'Crunch points in writing essays', 5: WE, 5.1).

- **A specific set of criteria** generated by the group of students for this task and their own assessment of how they fared. (For an example of this, see the feedback section for 4: WR, 2.2).

- **An assessment sheet** specifying the criteria on which the piece will be assessed (see the examples in Section 2.4 above). Students record a grade for themselves for each of the various criteria on the assessment sheet, add a comment, and attach the sheet to the work they hand in. Tutors record their assessment and comments on the same sheet and return it to the students with the marked piece of work. (See the feedback section for 4: WR, 2.2, for an example of a sheet used in this way in an engineering course.)

- **A reflective statement**, in which the student records their approach to the task:

Self-assessment

How I approached this piece of work:

What I found easy or difficult to do:

What I have learnt:

If I were to do a similar piece again, what I would do differently:

I would like particular feedback on:

2.9   Setting up peer tutoring

Students can often help each other to improve their writing. Peer tutoring can take various forms.

Co-consulting

Students can simply help each other in pairs, swapping drafts, reading them and then taking turns to suggest improvements or even redrafting alternative sentences or sections.

Supplemental instruction (SI)

SI is a formalized system of peer tutoring, in which students are encouraged to find answers to their problems from within a group of fellow students. The group is led by a student who has already successfully completed the course or module, and whose task is to facilitate the group process, not teach the subject. The system was developed in the early 1970s in the States as a response to courses seen as difficult. It has also been used in this country as a way of offering additional support to students on courses with high student numbers.

In being offered to all students on the course, SI is not, and is not seen to be, remedial or didactic teaching. The SI leaders are given training in how to run the sessions, and to turn the issues and problems students bring to the session into the agenda for that session. Students who take advantage of SI seem to improve their performance on that module by a full grade, and the benefits carry over to subsequent modules where the teaching style and tutors' expectations of students are similar. The benefits to the SI leaders is in terms of their own development in interpersonal skills, management and organization, and in revising and deepening their own understanding of the subject.

Swap shop

At the end of tutorials or group work sessions, five minutes can be put aside for peer support with writing. Students can be asked to offer tips and to seek help with requests. A tip might be:

> I've found that when I get stuck with writing – like when I realize I've been sitting for 20 minutes without writing a word – if I just ramble out loud into my Walkman it usually gets me unstuck. I often don't need to listen to the tape sometimes. Make sure no one else is in the room because you often talk complete garbage before it becomes usable!

2.10 Self-instruction

In higher education, students spend much of their time in self-instruction in their subject area, and have, presumably, developed a degree of proficiency at it. Self-instruction in writing skills, however, is another matter; even in courses where a study skills book is top of the reading list, tutors report the frustrations of trying to get students to read it. Evidently, study and writing skills are seen as a low priority by students under pressure from their other subjects – probably the very students who most need to work on these skills.

Why is this? A speculative answer to the question might be that students feel that study skills advice in books does not apply to them. Even where the strategies or advice is sound, they have a point – why spend time working through a detailed example on a subject of no relevance or interest, or where the advice turns out to be slightly at odds with the preferences of the particular tutor? They are also right on another level: it is notoriously hard to identify a transferable skill you have, harder still to see how you acquired it, and well nigh impossible to see how following an unfamiliar process will lead to a skill you do not have! Students' complaints about relevance – whether articulated or implicit through their inaction – need to be addressed if they are to be motivated to commit the time and effort to self-instruction.

While this pack cannot hope to overcome all these pitfalls, below are some approaches to using the material to minimize the student reaction 'It's not for me . . .'

Run a key activity in class

This might be a substantial activity you decide to adopt as part of the course material (such as the workshops in 2: UD), or an approach you integrate into your existing pattern of teaching – such as analysing essay questions, or drawing up instant essay plans (5: WE, 3.1–3.5). The material in the guides acts as a back up, a reference point, and reinforcement of work done in class.

Make specific referrals

If you refer students to a specific chapter or section, they are more likely to do the work than if you make a general recommendation. An exam strategy (5: WE, 4.9), how to draw charts (2: UD, 4) and how to write a paragraph (1: EWS, 7.3; 5: WE, 5.3), are examples of specific references you might make.

The **blueprints** are designed for quick reference on formats:

* three formats for scientific reports in 3: S&T, 5.1, 5.2 and 5.3

* other formal reports in 4: WR, 4

* how to plan an essay in 5: WE (judgement essays in 3.6 and factual essays in 3.8).

If a specific referral is linked to a class initiative, the chances of a student following up and completing the activity are obviously much greater.

Use the material as a rehearsal

You can then run an equivalent activity with your own material. It is a positive advantage to do a dry run on, for example, writing introductions and conclusions and other aspects of essay writing using material that is unfamiliar to the student, followed by material from the student's subject. Students are quick to see the structures common to different contexts for writing (5: WE, 5.2 and 5.7).

Exploit the link between the Tutor Manual and the Student Guides

If you decide to use a strategy outlined in the Tutor Manual, you will find that it is well supported by the material in the Student Guides. Even where your approach to, say, establishing assessment criteria is different in detail, the material in the relevant section of the guides will provide a focus for a discussion of what you are aiming to do and why you are doing it in this way.

Give credit for completing specified sections

If you are able to do this within an existing course or module – true 'open learning' – it may help student motivation. You need to:

* be sure the materials satisfy your specific objectives for the student(s)

* work out how much study time you expect a section to take, specify the form and detail of the written outcomes you reckon, and agree this with the student(s).

2.11 Running writing skills sessions and courses

When you have identified a need to develop students' writing skills, your next problem is how to do it. If you have identified a need shared by a particular group of students, you will have to find a way of adding some kind of provision to this year's busy schedule. If you can anticipate the need to build the development of writing skills into the course programme, for next year's students, for instance, then you have more options in the type of provision you can make. This section outlines the options you might consider.

Building writing skills into generic skills modules

Generic skills modules are designed to introduce students to how to study the specific discipline. The development of writing skills is placed clearly in the context of the academic processes and outcomes required by that discipline. This approach to developing writing skills overcomes many of the concerns of tutors about the reluctance of students to commit time and effort to self-instruction, or to following up tutors' feedback on their work. It provides a positive experience of academic study in the subject and a sound foundation for their future studies.

Generic skills modules are increasingly being introduced as assessed modules which count towards the students' first-year marks. The policy of the University of Northumbria at Newcastle is to establish a generic skills module in every subject area; 'Geographical Enquiry' and 'Introduction to Sociology' run at Oxford Brookes University.

The outline below is of the generic skills module in social science at the University of Hertfordshire. The content is social science, but the focus of attention is the process and skill of writing, and there is plenty of scope for tutors to work on writing skills specific to the discipline. Writing is seen as part of the overall process of scholarship, including researching, reading and evaluating outcomes, not as an isolated skill.

Running writing skills modules and short courses

Points to think about if you are planning to run a writing skills module or short course include:

- how to assess it

- how to accredit it within the student's overall programme

- the skills you want the students to develop

- the specific forms of writing you want students to be able to use

- the content you plan to use as the context for developing these skills.

Writing skills modules aim to develop writing skills with groups of students who share an unfamiliarity with the forms and conventions of academic writing but are drawn from a range of subjects or disciplines. International students, mature students, or students with an alternative entry route are examples of groups who may be drawn together in this way. The problem with modules or short courses of this sort can be to ensure that the forms and conventions taught are relevant to the range of disciplines from which students are drawn, and to work with content that students can see is relevant to their needs.

This series can be used to resource sessions in a module or course of this sort. Materials are drawn from a wide area of subjects and the comparative approach aims to make the range of experiences students bring to the module a resource rather than a constraint. The chapter on process in each Student Guide is designed to highlight the shared features that underpin writing. Guidance on form is given in the following chapters to encourage student writers to see the final stages of drafting a piece of work as a matter of tailoring content to the present purpose and audience. This approach is shared by all the Student Guides, but is perhaps shown most clearly in 3: S&T, 3 and 4.

Whatever the linguistic background of students taking these modules, it is well worth looking at how you might adapt some of the strategies current in materials designed for advanced language learners. (See Further reading.)

Running writing skills sessions

These can be helpful in

- establishing writing skills in courses where no other specific provision exists

- providing a specific input at a particular point in the learning or writing cycle that raised problems in the past

- raising awareness of whole groups or cohorts to some aspect of writing skills (e.g., formats for reports, essay planning), with follow-up for small groups or individuals as appropriate.

The essential point about any short input into courses running with a different agenda is to discuss the specification with the tutor(s) involved so that you tailor it totally to the needs of the students. This is a form of consultancy, and if you do not design your sessions to meet the needs of your two key client groups, tutor and students, your contribution runs the risk of being seen as irrelevant or off-beam.

Running writing skills sessions and short courses involves a lot of work in proportion to the amount of time you spend with the group. Before the session you need to

- find out precisely what problems led the tutor to approach you to ask for an input, and what kind of input they think might be useful. Examples of strategies and materials you might adapt can be helpful in translating a concern into a proposal.

- ask to see course materials – reading tasks, written assignments set, marking scheme – to get an idea of the demands of the course and timing of assignments in relation to the sessions.

- ask for examples of a cross-section of student writing and a model of good practice.

Then go away and draw up your outline for the sessions, and consult the tutor again before you run them.

After a session it is essential to ask for feedback from the participants and the tutor(s). Harder to arrange, but equally important, is feedback at a later stage, perhaps after the particular task has been completed, marked and returned to students, to find out if the sessions translated into better writing in the long run. This feedback can be used as an element in planning the nature and timing of the skills input next time around.

2.12 Using specialist help

Some students may have particular difficulties with writing that go beyond the scope of the strategies suggested in this manual, and beyond the expertise – or time – you have to offer. These difficulties may involve dyslexia, writing in English as a second (or third) language, basic literacy or extreme anxiety. You need to recognize the difficulties such students present and refer them to specialists for practical support or counselling as appropriate. There may be self-instructional materials in print or on computer, support groups, or organized sessions on particular topics or to meet special needs. At some institutions students are able to gain credit for work done in this way, and students may be allowed concessions in assessed tasks – to use a word processor in exams, for example. It is helpful if you can make an accurate referral, if not to a named individual, at least to a central point, for example checking the title, phone number or drop-in hours of the Student Services Officer, or equivalent post holder in your institution.

Perhaps the most puzzling of these categories for most tutors is that of 'dyslexia', a term widely used but little understood. What is the difference between a student with poor spelling, who needs to go and learn some spelling rules, and a student with 'specific learning difficulties', a more accurate way of describing dyslexia? This is not the place for a discussion of this, nor for suggesting DIY diagnosis, but simply to put forward a few pointers as a prompt for when to refer a student to a specialist for assessment.

Advice given to readers of dyslexic writing may be along these lines:

Dyslexia is often thought of as a question of poor spelling. Spelling errors are certainly one of the more obvious symptoms of specific learning difficulties (dyslexia), but the problems with sequencing and short-term memory that lead to poor spelling can also lead to difficulties with sentence structure, sorting information, word order, or to strange and convoluted syntax. Dyslexic students often get lost in their writing, especially when there is a keyword common to two or more main points that they want to make. They may move from one point into the middle of another point they were intending to make . . .

. . . Sometimes the reader can see what the student is trying to say, even if the expression is awkward, in incomplete sentences, or with unfinished trains of thought. In other cases, however, it is not clear to the reader what the student is trying to say . . .

The problem for the tutor is to distinguish between students who have a serious difficulty and need help in overcoming it or accommodating it, and those that need to work on some specific aspect of their basic writing skills, however this is done. Where problems are so severe that the writer fails to communicate meaning to a willing reader, you will probably have little hesitation in making the referral. The problem arises when the line between specific difficulties and common errors is finer.

How do you react to the following three extracts from student writing? Would you refer any of these to a specialist for assessment and possible support?

Extract 1

Paul Unsheild reveals this plurality of conceptualization is related to systems which are mutualy incompatible and associated with the presence in society of groups which have different ideologies. He shows this historicaly (1986) Conceptions differ between age groups, and differ greatly trans culturaly or ethnicaly. (Currer and Stacey 1986) The differences between lay and professional perspectives on health are most pertinantly revealed by Ann Oakley (1986) in

Extract 2

Caring for a patient does not stop at the bedside of the patient the family has to be considered, if a patient were to die the nurse would have to draw on her sociological, psychological and biological knowledge in order to comfort the family explaining why death occured and understanding what the family are going through after the death ~~the~~ the nurse draws on the sociological ~~knowledge~~, remembering how humans view ~~death~~ so as to council the ~~pat~~ family who almost became the patient, ~~even~~ the nurse may even disclose personal experiences to the family showing the tradegy happens to everyone, as a social worker would do when councilling this 'disclosure' of personal experiences breaksdown a wall between two relative strangers building up trust.

CONSTRUCTION PROCEDURE

The construction started as planned, with one person cutting and twisting the polythene while the other two mapped out and cut the plywood

The towers were completed on schedual with little problem. However the main bridge section was failing to take shape due to the fact that the cables were not sticky enough to hold the pieces of wood together. To try and overcome this problem all 3 members worked on the bridge at once. Trying to hold it together long enough for it to be bound by the polythene loops.

Unfortunally while the structure was being made some of the polythene bands were pulled to tight, making the structure buckle because of the Buckling the vertical pieces of wood in the main section was noted. This

Desigied   Acrual

resulted in pusing the cables into the side wall producing even more deformation.

Alot of time was spent trying to rectify this problem but to no aval. Because of the resulting time lost, only two surspension cables could be attached. One at either end, with then being tied together underneath the bridge.

Comment

Extract 1

This student seems fluent and in control of the complex process of drawing together references to different sources, but presents surprising irritants in the path of the reader through minor spelling mistakes. A closer look shows that four of the five spelling mistakes in this short extract follow the same pattern – failure to double the 'l' in forming an adverb: *mutual/mutually, historical/historically,* etc.

Verdict: no referral. Tutor points it out – student learns it fast! (This example is used in 1:EWS, 8.2.)

Extract 2

This is one long incoherent sentence with a mass of incoherent thoughts! This extract is used as the basis for an exercise in sentence structure in 1: EWS, 5.4, but in the next assignment the student writes the problem may be better tackled in the thinking and planning stage of the essay. As a first step, it may be worth asking this student to submit their next essay in two or more stages: first the plan, then the draft (for self-assessment or peer feedback? See Section 2.8 above), before presenting the final version. If these problems persist, then you may need to explore what support in writing skills you might refer the student to. This does not seem to be a case for referral for specialist assessment in the first instance, but there is a need for specific follow-up work.

Extract 3

At first sight, this looks like a mediocre piece of work. A closer look reveals

- surprising errors in spelling: *lables/labels*; *peices/pieces*; *to/too*; *desiged/designed*; *pusing/pushing*; *no aval/no avail*; and so on. Some of these flout spelling 'rules' (i before e except after c), others appear eccentric and nonsensical

- erratic sentence structure: *Trying to hold it all together . . .*; *One at either end . . .*

- short paragraphs, suggesting insufficiently developed ideas or lack of structure for ideas.

Although this student's problems may at first glance seem indistinguishable from those of others showing a high level of inaccuracy, this student should be referred to a specialist for assessment. Errors that do not seem to 'make sense' to the tutor/reader may indicate specific learning difficulties – which is for the specialist to determine and address. Despite the catalogue of errors in this short extract, the writing presents the reader with no difficulty in understanding what the writer is trying to say. The student coped well with the substantive task (the bridge assignment; see 3: S&T, 2.2; 4: WR, 2.1). The first steps towards taking positive action may be as simple as learning to type and use a spellcheck.

The key point in deciding whether to refer students for specialist assessment is to consider whether you are left with a sense of discrepancy in your assessment of the student: discrepancy between their performance in class and their written work; discrepancy in their performance between one type of activity and another. Even this is not a hard and fast rule. Other students and groups of students (such as mature students) may underperform in written tasks, but you should see rapid progress where students have no additional difficulties to overcome.

If you do find yourself marking the work of a dyslexic student, your institution may be able to offer you some guidelines on how to approach this constructively. Below is a summary of guidelines offered to tutors at Oxford Brookes University. This booklet offers fuller help on each point, and a rationale, or explanation, for each piece of advice.

Marking the work of dyslexic students

> **A busy marker's brief summary**
>
> 1 Read fast, looking for ideas, understanding and knowledge.
>
> 2 Make constructive comments.
>
> 3 Be explicit. Explain your comments clearly, and write legibly.
>
> 4 Say what you are marking for. If you mark only for the ideas, say so.
>
> 5 Use two pens (neither red), one for ideas, the other for language.
>
> 6 Be selective. Do not correct everything and be prepared to explain what is wrong.
>
> 7 Be sensitive. Many dyslexic students have been hurt by lack of understanding in the past.
>
> *(Adapted from Guidelines of Good Practice with Respect to Marking the Work of Dyslexic Students)*

The object of this exercise is not to develop skills in DIY diagnosis of dyslexia, but to highlight some features of student writing about which tutors would wish to seek a specialist view. If in doubt, make the referral for assessment; whatever the outcome, it will be more positive for the student than a string of inexplicably low grades.

2.13 Towards the development of a comprehensive writing policy

The strategies to promote good student writing outlined so far can be introduced by individual tutors or groups of tutors. These strategies are likely to be more effective when they are implemented as part of a comprehensive approach.

Comprehensive strategies involve the commitment of all the tutors across a section of the institution – department, field, subject – to delivering particular sets of transferable skills through the courses they teach. For writing skills, the aim would be to identify those skills students need to succeed in the curriculum, and ensure that they are taught, practised, assessed and accredited at appropriate points through the course. In this way, students will only be assessed on skills they have had the opportunity to acquire as part of a planned programme.

The case study below shows how this approach has been developed in the geology field at Oxford Brookes University. Extracts are reproduced with thanks to Richard D'Lemos of the Geology Department.

Case study

Step 1: What skills?

The department identified the skills, both transferable and discipline specific, they wanted all graduates to possess.

Step 2: How to develop the skills?

Staff considered their courses and identified the modules in which these skills were already taught. They then worked out how they might formalize this process, to agree the detail of a programme by which the skills might be

    T   taught

    P   practised

    A   assessed.

The result is the skills matrix, from which an extract is shown below:

	8301	8304	8308		8307	8364	proj
SELF-MANAGEMENT							
clarify personal views							
set personal objectives		P					P A
manage time & tasks	P		T		P	P	A
evaluate own performance		P	T		PA	T	A
LEARNING SKILLS							
independently & cooperatively	P		T	TA	A	TA	A
library & information skills			T	PA		TA	A
academic skills	T	TA	TA	P		TA	A
evaluate learning strategies	P	P	T				P
information technology							P
COMMUNICATION							
appropriate language	TA		TA	TA	PA	PA	A
appropriate media		TA	TA		A	PA	A
listen actively			TA	P			
persuade rationally		TA	TA	P		TA	A
TEAMWORK							
take responsibility		TA		P			P
take initiative & lead							
supportive roles within teams			TA				
negotiate, assert & respect			TA			T	
evaluate team performance			TA			TA	
PROBLEM-SOLVING							
analyse	TA	TA	TA	PA	A	TA	A
think laterally	P	TA	TA	P	A	TA	A
identify strategic options		TA		P		P	A
evaluate success of strategies		T				P	A
DISCIPLINARY/PROFESSIONAL							
geological reports		TA			TA	PA	A
synthesize & evaluate databases	TA	TA	TA		PA	PA	A
extrapolate from 2D to 3D		TA	TA		TA		A
formulate & test hypotheses		TA		TA	TA	PA	A
geological histories & timescales	TA	TA	TA	TA			A
terms, definitions & classification	TA	TA	TA	TA		PA	A
safe working in field & lab			T				P
instrumentation handling							T
observe & record in the field	T		TA				A
observe & record in the lab	T			TA			A
awareness of geology in society			P	T			
understand landscape processes	TA	TA		T	T		A
construct & interpret maps			TA		T		A
vocational skills					T		TA A

Step 3: When to deliver?

A sequence for delivering these transferable skills through the three years of the modular degree has also been developed. This ensures that the foundations of the skill have been developed before further demands are made. The progression in writing skills (highlighted in the diagram overleaf) shows an advance from 'Writing and illustrating' in the first year, to 'Scientific reportage' in the second, and 'Effective communication' in the context of project work in the third.

TRANSFERABLE SKILLS TRAINING AND APPRAISAL POINTS
GEOLOGY DOUBLE FIELDS

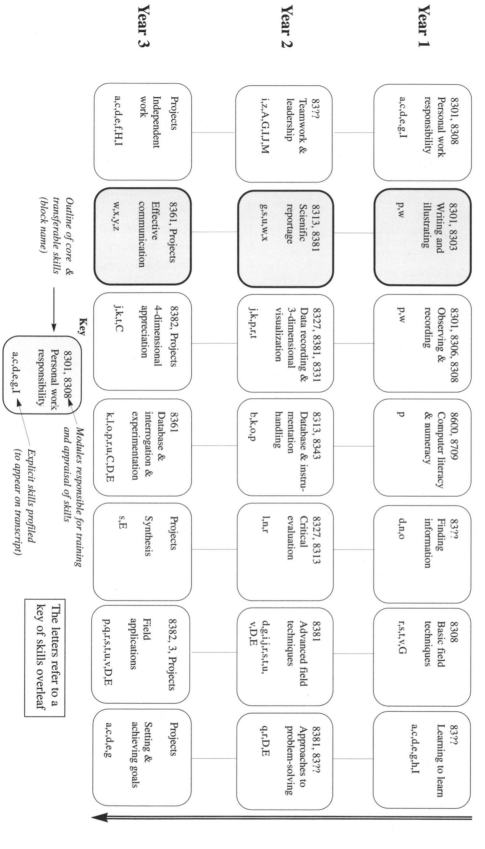

Year 1

8301, 8308
Personal work
responsibility

a,c,d,e,g,I

8301, 8303
Writing and
illustrating

p,w

8301, 8306, 8308
Observing &
recording

p,w

8600, 8709
Computer literacy
& numeracy

p

83??
Finding
information

d,n,o

8308
Basic field
techniques

r,s,t,v,G

83??
Learning to learn

a,c,d,e,g,h,I

Year 2

83??
Teamwork &
leadership

i,z,A,G,I,J,M

8313, 8381
Scientific
reportage

g,s,u,w,x

8327, 8381, 8331
Data recording &
3-dimensional
visualization

j,k,p,r,t

8313, 8343
Database & instru-
mentation
handling

b,k,o,p

8327, 8313
Critical
evaluation

l,n,r

8381
Advanced field
techniques

d,g,i,j,r,s,t,u,
v,D,E

8381, 83??
Approaches to
problem-solving

q,r,D,E

Year 3

Projects
Independent
work

a,c,d,e,f,H,I

8361, Projects
Effective
communication

w,X,y,z

8382, Projects
4-dimensional
appreciation

j,k,t,C

8361
Database &
interrogation &
experimentation

k,l,o,p,r,u,C,D,E

Projects
Synthesis

s,E

8382, 3, Projects
Field
applications

p,q,r,s,t,u,v,D,E

Projects
Setting &
achieving goals

a,c,d,e,g

Key

*Outline of core &
transferable skills
(block name)*

*Modules responsible for training
and appraisal of skills*

8301, 8308
Personal work
responsibility

a,c,d,e,g,I

*Explicit skills profiled
(to appear on transcript)*

The letters refer to a
key of skills overleaf

Key

Personal skills

Manage personal learning development

a	-	clarify personal values
b	-	consider career options
c	-	evaluate own performance
d	-	set objectives for self
e	-	manage own time and tasks
f	-	manage own feelings
g	-	work to deadlines

Study skills

h	-	use a range of learning skills
i	-	work cooperatively

Use a range of thinking styles

j	-	conceptual
k	-	analytic
l	-	strategic
m	-	symbolic

Use information handling skills

n	-	use library skills
o	-	use information technology
p	-	record and organize information

Use academic skills

q	-	research
r	-	analyse
s	-	synthesize
t	-	interpret
u	-	integrate
v	-	hypothesize

Communication skills

w	Write and speak effectively
x	Use appropriate written language and format
y	Present ideas to different audiences
z	Persuade rationally
A	Listen actively
B	Use interviewing skills

Creative and problem-solving skills

C	Think laterally
D	Use problem-solving strategies
E	Develop, implement and evaluate ideas, processes and products

Interpersonal skills

F	Establish relationships
G	Work productively in different teams
H	Take initiative
I	Take responsibility
J	Lead others
K	Negotiate
L	Assert own feelings
M	Evaluate team performance

This example of the development of a comprehensive policy for developing transferable skills – to which writing is central – illustrates the advantages of such a system. Comprehensive strategies are

- built into the way modules are designed and taught, rather than being left to the initiative of conscientious tutors

- built into the assessment system so that students cannot avoid gaining practice and skills and are explicitly rewarded for developing writing skills

- well documented: students can see models of good writing, how they are supposed to write, how to improve

- implemented in a consistent way by all tutors, through the adoption, for example, of a consistent set of criteria for written work across all modules

- allocated classroom time – an indication of their importance

- progressive: basic writing skills are developed early in Year 1, and more sophisticated writing skills are developed over the three years in planned stages

- responsive to student diversity and special needs

- geared to effective and early diagnosis of problems. This allows targeted and timely remedial support so that problems with writing do not undermine the student's achievement in successive modules.

This chapter has outlined some of the steps tutors can take to develop students' writing. The focus has been on strategic action to be taken by tutors as individuals, by groups of teaching staff, or across a wide swathe of the university to establish the framework in which students write. The next chapter suggests ways of working with the material in the Student Guides as supporting action, and to develop specific writing skills with individual students or groups of students.

Using the Student Guides

The Student Guides are designed primarily as an accessible user-friendly resource for students working on their own in order to improve particular aspects of their writing. If, however, they are used in conjunction with some of the strategies outlined in the previous chapter, the material will be seen as more relevant and will be more effective – because students are more likely to understand the purpose underpinning a particular activity. This chapter is designed to give an overview of the content of the guides and some suggestions as to how material might be adapted for use with groups of students.

The design of the Student Guides

There are five Student Guides in the series. These are

1 *Essential Writing Skills* (1: EWS)

2 *Using Data* (2: UD)

3 *Scientific and Technical Writing* (3: S&T)

4 *Writing Reports* (4: WR)

5 *Writing Essays* (5: WE).

The abbreviations used in the text for cross-referencing are shown in brackets, and section references in the individual guides are shown as numbers following the title reference. For example: '5: WE, 5.6' is a reference to Student Guide 5, *Writing Essays*, Chapter 5, Section 6, 'Using other people's ideas'.

The guides provide models of a range of the written work students are most often required to produce and help through the process of producing them. The thinking is that, if students engage in the process and see this formative stage as a legitimate part of their writing task, they are more likely to understand why the end-product has to have certain features and to put in the necessary effort to ensure that it does. From this angle, issues of correctness, whether of overall form (of an essay or report) or accuracy (of spelling, punctuation or citing references), can be seen as an aspect of effective communication: a piece of writing has a particular form because it is produced for a particular purpose and for a particular audience.

To encourage a feeling of familiarity with the processes shared to a greater or lesser extent by any writing task, the core chapters of the guides follow the same pattern:

- strategic thinking

- glimpsing the process

- writing the . . . (report, essay).

Guides 4 and 5 end with a chapter which anticipates tutor initiatives in setting written tasks with a wider range of formats than those featuring in the titles of the guides.

3.1 Using Student Guide 1: *Essential Writing Skills*

It is a commonplace that the more self-evident the skill, the harder it is to teach and learn. Sentence structure, for example, is hard to teach in higher education because tutors do not have the time to engage in this time-consuming process; they do not have the skills to teach at foundation level, and perhaps have a lingering resentment that this sort of teaching is necessary in HE. But if the skills are not taught, how are students to learn?

The reasons why students find these skills difficult to learn mirror the reasons why they are hard to teach: it is a time-consuming process and students with such difficulties are likely to be under pressure from other quarters; they cannot address the problem unaided because its roots lie far back in their own learning experiences, and they are uncomfortable about the existence of such fundamental difficulties in the context in which they now find themselves. Nevertheless, some mutually acceptable way forward in teaching and learning essential writing skills needs to be found, because until the problem is addressed too many students will fail to exploit the link between thinking and writing, and their own academic success.

Student Guide 1 is designed to contribute to this learning process and to meet some of the different needs users will bring to it:

- quick reference 'How to . . .' sections on rules and usage, where appropriate

- a fuller explanation of 'rules'

- the opportunity to observe the rules at work in other people's writing, and to practise and apply them in materials and contexts supplied

- templates for writing where appropriate (e.g., paragraphs)

- worked examples of 'How to . . .' placed in a context designed to enable the reader to understand why things have to be done in a particular way. The fullest example of this is Chapter 9, in which how to reference is placed in the context of why referencing is important – leading to the core of the academic process.

Why is so much space devoted to explaining points that people can be told in two minutes – how to write a sentence, how to reference using the Harvard style, how to use commas and so on? The reason is that tutors may impart the information in two minutes, but do students learn in two minutes? For those aspects of basic skills in writing that persist as problems into higher education, the evidence suggests that they do not. This is why this guide proceeds through explanation as well as offering simple 'How to . . .' sections. In some places this is brief, and in others (such as Chapter 9) it reaches into the nature and purpose of academic discourse.

Little of this will be found in the text, but you will see the footprints of such thinking in the practical explanations and exercises in the guide. Most chapters start with a consideration of the needs of the reader – expressed bluntly in the form of (genuine) tutor comments on students' work. In this way, work on the particular aspect of writing explored in the chapter is placed firmly in the context of effective writing for the audiences students most often face – tutors and examiners. For some students the 'How to . . .' sections will be enough. Others will need to take the time to work through the explanations and thought processes to make sense of the 'How to . . .' sections. These are the students who may need your time and support.

3.1A   Ask key questions (2.1)

The same strategic approach to considering the needs of the audience and the purpose of writing before setting out on a writing task is used in this guide as in the others in the series. It sets questions of style, accuracy and 'correctness' in the context of the wider purpose the writer wants to achieve. You could supplement it by highlighting the particular requirements of the form of academic writing you have set on this occasion.

3.1B   Judging the context (2.2)

This is the first of many occasions in the guide on which the student is referred to the extracts in the appendix for an activity. These are exercises in applying the principles outlined in the text. Because it is a self-contained activity it is suitable for use with groups of students, including those drawn from a range of subject areas.

3.1C   Gathering information (3.1)

This overview of using sources is brief because here it is presented as part of a process. You may wish to refer students who need more guidance in the use of academic sources to Chapter 9. All the guides in the series focus on the processes at work in presenting assignments in particular forms.

It is worth pointing out to students that it is useful to become familiar with the seven points to look for in recording the details of a written source. The order in which they are given here translates directly into the order in which they are presented in the Harvard system of referencing.

3.1D   Writing the first draft (3.2)

This section introduces the notion of writing for a reader as the context for considering issues of accuracy and 'correctness'. This is a helpful approach in convincing students that it is not acceptable to hand in the first draft of a piece of writing – professionals don't do it!

3.1E   Presenting your work (3.3)

It is a good idea if students know the range of formats that is acceptable for each piece of work. Specific aspects of presentation may be assessed if appropriate. The use of a word processor, for example, may be required and assessed on some occasions, practised on others, or left optional.

3.1F   Using apostrophes (Ch. 4)

This chapter places the simple 'How to . . .' format in the context of distractions in the path of the reader, and includes exercises on identifying and explaining usage. It can be used as open learning material for students working on their own, although a referral direct to the chapter would help motivation.

3.1G   Writing sentences (Ch. 5)

The approach in this guide is to present punctuation as the means by which structure is given to words to 'make sense'. This is why the 'rule boxes' on the use of particular pieces of punctuation are placed within chapters on sentence structure. Chapter 5 is designed as a resource for students who have been told to 'Find a book that explains how to . . .'. The explanations and exercises are very basic, but look at the nature of a sentence from several angles. The best, of course, is a gut feeling that something is or is not right . . .

3.1H   Writing complex sentences (6.1)

This section includes clear 'rule boxes' for the use of commas, colons, semi-colons and bullet points, and opportunities to apply the rules and see them at work. It ends with the suggestion that students look critically at one passage of their reading matter in any reading session to try and explain the use of each mark of punctuation used. This is good advice but it may cause problems, because much of what they read, academic as well as leisure reading, will be badly written and contain basic errors! You need to be prepared for this and to suggest examples of good writing as a model. *The Economist* generally lives up to its reputation for being a well written periodical.

3.1I   How to write paragraphs – the paragraph plan (7.3)

This simple paragraph plan is enormously useful to students, and you may wish to use it in a number of ways. You may either simply show it, or use it as a template for an evaluation of effective writing in your subject. Your material might be a paragraph of student writing or a text in your subject. You can then discuss the ways in which the writing does – or does not – follow the plan, and the effect of doing/not doing so.

Readers of academic work expect it to be presented in a form that makes use of the conventions of academic discourse, to which the structure of argument is crucial. Where the argument appears unclear, unsupported or of dubious relevance to the title it is often, quite simply, a result of the writer's lack of skill in how to make paragraphs work to promote their purpose. In practical terms this tends to be:

Problem	Remedy
• Lack of topic sentence	Add one to – express the main idea – make the link with the paragraph before – make the link with the title.
• One-sentence 'paragraphs'	Add definition, explanation, illustrations, and stress that these must be commented on.
• Lack of concluding sentence	Add one – to show the progression of the argument, and links with the topic sentence and the title.

These are the skills in writing paragraphs that Chapter 7 is designed to develop through instruction (the 'paragraph plan'), observation, analysis and practice.

3.1J   Good spelling (Ch. 8)

This chapter is designed to speak directly to the individual student concerned about spelling. It is arranged as a checklist of the strategies students might employ to develop their own 'spelling awareness' and from there to work out remedies. You may wish to draw the attention of students to individual patterns of misspelling (8.2) and add to the tutors' hit list (8.8). For all-round entertainment on the effectiveness of spellchecks as a substitute for checking work, the extract in 8.9 is good value.

You will also want to be on the look-out for the occasional student whose problems with spelling seem to go beyond the strategies suggested in this chapter. See section 2.12 above, 'Using specialist help', for prompts as to when you might wish to refer a student for specialist advice and assistance.

3.1K   Using sources in academic work (Ch. 9)

Chapter 9 is designed to generate an understanding of the place of sources in academic work, since this is a prerequisite to both fluent discussion of different authorities and accurate referencing. You may wish to develop this into a more explicit discussion of the context in which students write, and the expectations of the particular writing community into which the student has entered. Brookes and Grundy (1990) give a useful outline of these issues and practical exercises to highlight the processes and assumptions at work. Although the authors designed the materials for use with non-native English speakers, their insights are helpful and the exercises non-didactic and adaptable.

3.1L   A glimpse at the academic process (9.1)

'Was Malthus right about population?', the essay title used here to illustrate the research process and the mechanics of how to refer to other people's writing, is also used to illustrate the blueprint for a 'judgement essay' in 5: WE, 3.5.

This title was chosen because of its direct phrasing, and because few students will have any prior knowledge of the subject – an advantage where the focus is on skills, not content.

3.1M   Writing your bibliography (9.3)

This section gives a bare outline of the mechanics of recording references accurately. It is not designed to be comprehensive. Students will need to be directed to sources, or offered models for how to refer to sources, that differ in detail from the models here, using the style favoured in the school or department.

3.1N   The FOG index (10.1)

This is proposed more as entertainment at other writers' expense than as a serious tool for analysing writing, but it can be used for the latter. The remedy for high scores is invariably to write shorter sentences and use shorter words – the central message of this Student Guide.

3.1O   Using Grammatik (10.2)

In the near future, software packages such as this will become much more sensitive and intelligent. Meanwhile, they are worth playing with; they have serious potential as a tool in teaching and learning about writing.

3.1P   Non-sexist writing (10.3)

All the Student Guides are written in accordance with the principles given here. The main use of this section is less to argue for this contemporary style in addressing the reader than to suggest acceptable ways of doing so, particularly in the use of pronouns.

3.2   Using Student Guide 2: *Using Data*

The material in this guide spans a great range of skills in understanding data and presenting and interpreting information. It is designed, on the one hand, to be a friendly first step for the data-phobe, and, on the other, to provide some rich pickings for students moving on to develop skills in interpretation, translation and use of evidence. The advantage of using material which has been selected and structured as this has is that it is coherent both in content and in the progression of skills. Because of the thematic links between one table and another, there is an in-built motivation to pursue an inquiry and reach some conclusions – about which students can then write.

The contexts in which students need to develop confidence in data presentation and interpretation are particularly wide ranging and include

- social science foundation courses

- study skills sessions and courses

- supporting workshops for students with non-traditional backgrounds

- writing skills courses for international and second language students. Material in numerical format is particularly useful with these students, as you can concentrate on the interpretation and writing without the barriers often presented by stimulus material in written format. The material doubles as an introduction to aspects of British life and society.

Of all the guides in the series, *Using Data* would most benefit from tutor selection and direction. The suggestions below focus on activities and materials that are particularly suitable for group work.

3.2A Setting out on an inquiry (2.1)

When they are about to set out on their own inquiry, it may be helpful to ask each student or group of students to draw up their own 'From idea to action' diagram, to record their thoughts on their first steps. You may decide to leave the form of this open to the students or suggest that they adopt the form below:

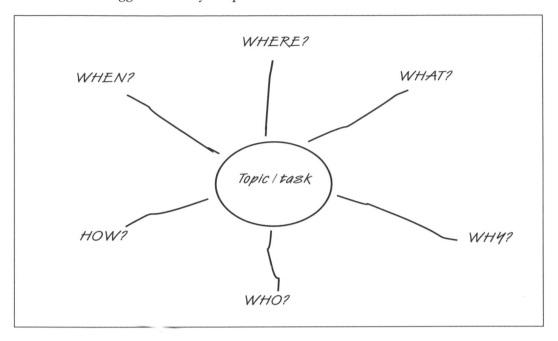

3.2B Ask questions about other people's data (2.2)

The same format for recording the answers to the 'key questions' can be used in relation to data students bring back from their researches. It is helpful to make this visual link between the process of generating data when you do it yourself and the processes that lie behind the data you first encounter in published form.

3.2C Wording a questionnaire (3.1)

This is the only section developed in any detail in the section 'Gathering data'. Only through trial, error and redrafting do students produce tightly worded questions in questionnaires. A brief discussion of these questions, comparing and contrasting open and closed questions, can be helpful in the early stages of compiling a questionnaire. Students can then use them as models if they decide to reword open questions as closed ones, or to reduce ambiguity.

3.2D A good table? (3.4.3)

The example given here is one of many that can be used to highlight features that help the reader seeking information from a table. By way of contrast, the table in 3: S&T, 3.2, is an example that is difficult to read and interpret. The activity in 3: S&T, 3.4, involves rotating the table through 90º to produce a much more readable, eye-friendly table.

3.2E The workshops

Each of the three workshops contains a substantial amount of material on topical but accessible subjects, from which you can make selections as appropriate, but which, if taken as a whole, build to a coherent and satisfying inquiry from data sources. There is a clear hierarchy of skills implied in the activities, with a parallel growth in the complexity of the material. The overall aim of the workshops is to enable students to gain the necessary skills and confidence to pursue independent inquiries drawing on information in numeric and graphical form.

Workshop 1: An Apple a Day . . .? (Ch. 4)

This workshop develops basic skills in how to present information based on data provided. Step-by-step guidance is given on drawing

- pie charts

- bar charts

- histograms.

The context is material on smoking and drinking habits taken from *An Apple a Day . . .? A Study of Lifestyles and Health* (1992), commissioned by Argyll and Clyde Health Board and undertaken by the Centre for Health Studies, University of Kent at Canterbury. The report is one of the models discussed in 4: WR.

One example of each of the three formats for charts (on smoking habits) is taken from the published report. Students are then given step-by-step guidance on how to draw another to the same model using given data (on drinking habits).

Workshop 2: Education in figures (Ch. 5)

This workshop on interpreting data and presenting information builds on the basic skills developed in Workshop 1. The context is a study of published government statistics showing trends in education, with a focus on higher education.

There is a clear progression of skills within the material, starting with interpretation of data in a table, based on highly specific ('In detail') questions. This is followed by structured activities in which the student is asked to select trends, to describe them in a range of visual forms, and to comment on what their charts reveal. The workshop ends with a suggestion for a more open-ended piece of writing (a short article) drawing on material which is by now thoroughly familiar. You may wish to extend the brief to students to include material taken from additional follow-up research. An up-date of the data presented offers a simple extension.

The workshop includes more suggestions for activities than any student would wish or need to follow up – which is where tutor direction is needed.

Workshop 3: The honourable lady was being selective . . . (Ch. 6)

The final workshop, on figures, facts and interpretation, should be a lot of fun for students who have developed confidence – and competence – in extracting and interpreting key figures from data. It demonstrates how flexible the truth can be in (political) argument and debate.

The focus here is on actively seeking out the facts about poverty and government policy in the face of sharply differing interpretations – the claims and counter-claims of two politicians, John Major, Conservative Prime Minister at the time, and Jean Corston, Labour MP for Bristol East. The balance in the text shifts again – more data, less direction, with an emphasis on drawing your own conclusions. The workshop ends with a suggestion for a written report using the question on which the workshop is based as the terms of reference. No indication of length is given – this is for the tutor to determine, depending on how you decide to use the material in the workshop.

3.3 Using Student Guide 3: *Scientific and Technical Writing*

This Student Guide has been devised primarily as a course companion for first-year or foundation science and technology students. Examples and contexts for activities are drawn from a cross-section of science and technical subjects. The emphasis is on core processes and skills and the choices to be made about the language, style and form of written English. The guide ends with three adaptable blueprints for scientific and technical report writing.

The guide is designed to be self-explanatory for students working on their own, with clear instructions, simple models, structured step-by-step activities and full feedback. Tutors may, however, wish to dip into it to highlight particular sections, guidance or approaches – or to point out where their own practice differs from the suggestions given. Links made in this way with the student's own course will also help to underline the guide's use as a course companion.

'Language in Science' (Chapter 4) is placed well into the book, so that students will have developed an understanding of the range of language appropriate in science through the variety of styles in the earlier extracts. The aim at this point is to fine-tune students to the particular requirements of their course.

3.3A Ask key questions (2.1)

The activity in this section is an exercise in using systematic questioning to clarify the tasks and processes in an engineering assignment. You may find it helpful to use these questions as a way of ensuring students have fully understood the implications of a task you set. Answers can be recorded in the form suggested in Section 3.2A above.

3.3B Look closely at assessment criteria (2.2)

This section is essentially about getting students to make full use of the guidance already available to them on the form and style required in their writing – reading between the lines to identify the assessment criteria. (See also Section 3.4A below.) There is a clear link with the 'key questions' approach in Section 3.3A above. You could underline this link by sketching points from your guidance under the headings below.

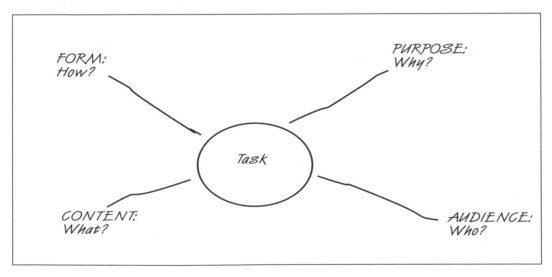

3.3C Labelling your work

To label work is a recurrent plea from science tutors! This section is designed to demonstrate why it is necessary to give the reader full information about a table. Students can use the 'five essential points' as a checklist for their own work and as a tool for checking their own grasp of detail when interpreting the results of others. The table at the end of Section 4.3 is an example of a well produced published table.

3.3D   Redraw a table (3.4)

This activity is to redraw the badly drawn table (supplied by a tutor!) in the extract from the student's work in Section 3.2. Once the students have run through this and progress to more complex examples, you may wish periodically to return to the issue of table design when you find examples of confusing or poorly designed tables.

3.3E   Working with tables and graphs (3.5)

This is the only extended activity in this guide, and takes the reader step by step through the stages of a simple lab experiment. It has been devised primarily to provide support materials for students who, for whatever reason, have missed out on this sort of basic scientific training. Although it is very simple, students who need such support would benefit from working with others. Equally, although full answers and explanations are given, you may wish to check students' work; print-based activities can only go so far!

That said, there may well be specific aspects you wish to draw to the attention of more proficient students, such as the annotated example of written comments on results – often a problem even with otherwise competent students.

3.3F   Structures for writing (4.2)

This section gives specific guidance (and illustration through activity) on how to organize text in response to some of the more frequently used instructions:

- define

- give an account of

- explain why

- compare and contrast

- describe.

Instructions used for essay writing, and blueprints for 'factual' and 'judgement' essays, are considered in 5: WE, 3.

3.3G   Choosing your style (4.4)

Tutor input would be helpful in this section, which is designed to make students aware of the range of styles acceptable in different scientific contexts:

- informal or formal?

- present record or past account?

- personal or impersonal?

- active or passive?

- everyday or technical language?

You may be able to use these headings as pegs or models for a discussion of the style in which you require students to submit work. Your input might take the form of one of the activities outlined in Section 2.5 above.

3.3H   Seeing through the FOG (4.5)

This is designed as light entertainment at the expense of a piece of writing you consider a model of how not to do it! It can help to make the point that, to write well as a scientist, you do not have to produce incomprehensible prose.

3.3I Writing reports (Ch. 5)

What do you want your students' work to look like? The blueprints presented in this chapter are designed as a quick reference point for models for the structure of scientific report writing. The three blueprints are for

- a standard lab report

- a formal practical report

- a technical report.

The consistency of form underlying the three is stressed, and the specific features of the more complex forms of reports are presented as variants on the form of the basic lab report. Your input as tutor is helpful in relating the guidance you give students elsewhere to the models suggested here. In this way, where there are differences of detail, the advice is more likely to be seen as complementary than as conflicting.

3.3J The cycle of inquiry (Ch. 6)

The diagram given here as a summary to the guide could equally well be used at the beginning of a cycle, to give students an overview of what they are embarking on. It is a fairly painless way of engaging students in reflecting on their individual learning process and of highlighting the correspondence with scientific process and the final written form of their work.

3.4 Using Student Guide 4: *Writing Reports*

Writing Reports has been devised as a stand-alone guide for students planning to produce their work in report form. The term 'report' covers a vast range of forms and styles of writing, to which individual tutors will wish to add their own specifications. To reflect this, the guide works largely through examples of reports taken in roughly equal proportions from student assignments and a range of work settings. In highlighting the differences in form and purpose between different reports, tutors may wish to use the material in the guide in a number of ways:

- to follow one or more of the five reports listed in Section 1.1 through the text

- to compare and contrast extracts in each section

- to use and adapt the blueprints outlined in Section 1.5 and detailed in Chapter 4.

In this way, students will be encouraged to see differences in style and form as stemming from the context of the report – not as conflicting advice.

3.4A Reports at work (1.2)

The activity here, based on actual comments by managers in a variety of fields, is designed to place in sharp focus how a report takes its form from the needs of the reader. The sketch in Section 3.3B above can be used as a skeleton for notes. In whatever form students choose to present their notes, it can be used as a simple note-taking exercise in sorting information. You can then ask students to repeat the layout they used for clarifying the context for the report they are about to write.

3.4B How reports are read (1.6)

This activity rapidly generates stimulus material for a consideration of the needs of different readers of a report. The items left blank are as revealing as those ticked.

3.4C The learning cycle (1.7 and 5.1) / the action cycle (5.2)

Many courses make explicit use of the learning cycle not only to prompt reflection on what students have learnt from a particular activity, but as a structure for forms of reflective writing, such as a reflective essay (set, for example, in an occupational therapy course) or a portfolio of individual learning (as in the hotel and catering module; see Section 3.5V below). This diagram of the learning process is particularly relevant to report writing. You can introduce it early, as a framework for the entire process, come back to it at the review stage (5.1), and use it show the link with action arising from the report (5.2). This pattern can be used in the review of an extended simulation of which report writing is a part.

3.4D Ask key questions (2.1)

The systematic approach to clarifying the health and safety task modelled in the guide can be used as a way of ensuring students have fully understood the implications of a task you set. Answers can be recorded in the form suggested in Section 3.2A above.

3.4E Looking at assessment criteria (2.3)

Section 2.4 above draws together references to examples of assessment criteria dispersed through the Student Guides. The purpose of the activity here is to encourage students to read between the lines of the guidance they already have, in whatever form it has been given. See Section 3.2B above.

3.4F Glimpsing the process (Ch. 3)

This chapter is designed to guide students through the processes normally invisible to tutors. If you want to monitor this process, or give yourself the option of intervening early if students are having a problem, you may wish to develop some of the suggestions for assessing the process given in Section 2.8.

3.4G Writing the report (Ch. 4)

This chapter gives straightforward 'How to . . .' guidance, working through the format of a longer report, section by section, based on Blueprint 2. Each section follows the same pattern: brief advice on what it should aim to achieve; several examples showing the solutions adopted by different report writers; and a prompt to student writers ('Your report') to determine the approach they will take and why.

The sections that cause most problems to student report writers are resourced to lend themselves to a brief focused activity in groups.

The introduction (4.4)

There are two activities based on a close examination of five extracts from reports. The activity placed before the extracts defines a purpose for reading – to be followed by a brief discussion. The activity given after the extracts provides a sharper focus for identifying the functions of an introduction as a lead-in to defining the purpose of the introduction in the students' report ('Your report'). These activities run together well in group work.

Conclusions and recommendations (4.6)

This exercise follows a similar pattern, and is designed to prompt discussion to clarify the difference between conclusions and recommendations. Students then move on to identify what is required of their own reports.

3.4H   Variations on the report form (5.3)

The forms outlined briefly in the Student Guide are designed to boost students' confidence when they are faced with a format that appears to be unfamiliar. The processes and skills are the same, but the form is tailored to a specific (defined) audience, closer to the context of the working world than the academic one. Various forms are listed in Section 2.3 above. The forms outlined here are

- report in role
- minutes
- minutes of a simulation
- presentation and handout
- workshop
- dossier.

Examples of two of these are given below.

A consequence of deciding to ask students to put together work in one of these alternative forms is to prompt tutors to produce much more detailed guidance on what is required than would often otherwise be the case. The need for this is self-evident: you have to plan the scenario, define (and perhaps document) the individual's role or task within it, and specify the form of the finished product. This process of defining the audience for a task, and the purpose the task is designed to fulfil, is in itself salutary; it does help to provide the framework for good writing.

Report in role

Below is an extract from a geography module handbook, in which the report is to be written from the perspective of an independent consultant.

TASK 3

You are required to adopt the role of independent consultant employed by the government to give it confidential advice on what strategy it should adopt at the enquiry into the Towyn Disaster. This evidence should be summarized in three succinct statements covering:

(i)   IMMEDIATE RESPONSIBILITY   Who should bear responsibility for the disaster at Towyn? What should the government's attitude be towards litigation procedures which might be started against (a) British Rail, (b) Colwyn Borough Council and (c) The National River Authority.

(ii) APPROPRIATE COASTAL DEFENCE STRUCTURES   What form of coastal defence would be most appropriate for the 1200 metres of coast line which needs to be upgraded at Towyn and how much approximately would your preferred scheme cost? You will find the details given in figure 5 useful here, although note that because the costings quoted are for 1986 they will need to be doubled to reflect today's costs.

(iii) LONG-TERM STRATEGY   In particular, what should the long-term objectives of a comprehensive coastal management plan for this stretch of coast include?

In practice the statement required is simply a precis of what the full report might contain. The total length of the three succinct statements should be 1000 words and must be handed in at the time of the seminar. The three sections need not necessarily be of equal length and may be augmented with diagrams or maps.

The extract from a student's response shows an attempt to follow the format of this form
of writing.

```
CONFIDENTIAL

For the attention of the Government
Location:  Towyn, Clwyd, North Wales
Date:  26th February 1990
Investigation:  Towyn Flood disaster
Company:  Independent Consultants
Report dated:  29th February 1990

Immediate Responsibility

After full investigation, all major parties
                        - British Rail
                        - National Rivers' Authority
                        - Colwyn Borough Council
                        - general public
involved in the incident, appear to have been negligent but to
differing degrees . . .
```

Workshop

Below are extracts showing 1) the learning outcomes towards which the students delivering this workshop were working, 2) the plan of a successful workshop delivered by two students and 3) the assessment sheet completed by the tutor after the workshop.

Extract 1

> **Workshop 5: Women in Europe**
>
> **Learning Outcomes**
>
> By the end of the workshop students should be able to:
>
> * identify EC initiatives intended to improve the position of women in employment
>
> * evaluate how effective these initiatives have been in the UK and other EC countries
>
> * suggest approaches which hospitality organizations could take to build on EC initiatives in order to improve the position of women within the hospitality industry.

Extract 2

WOMEN IN EUROPE
WORKSHOP PLAN
J.F. & T.K.

TIME	NOTES	WHO. VISUAL AIDS
10.15	Introduction	OHP
		T.K.
10.20	1) Reflection from work organization	T.K.
	2) Differences in pay between men and women	OHP
		T.K.
	3) Equal opportunity laws	OHP
		T.K.
	4) Gender pay equality evaluation	T.K.
10.35	5) Employment Rights Act 1993	OHP
		J.F.
	6) Childcare	OHP
		J.F.
	7) Equal opportunity survey	OHP
		J.F.
	8) Proportion of women in leading companies	OHP
		J.F.
10.50	9) Discussion: What can be done to improve women's position in the hospitality industry?	T.K.
		J.F.
		Group
11.05	10) Debate: Should women be treated equally?	Group
11.25	11) Conclusion	T.K.
		J.F.

Extract 3

Module 3173

Workshop Assessment

Names of Workshop Leaders _T.K. and J.F._

Scale: A = excellent B+ = very good B = good
        C = satisfactory F = poor

Mark

Workshop Plan (33.3%)

Organization of material (relevance, logical progression, conclusions) _B+_

Extent to which learning outcomes taken into account _B+_

Clarity (what, how, who, etc.) _B+_

Could have included more information re: what overheads were about, main learning points, etc.

Handling Workshop (33.3%)

Communication skills (verbal and non-verbal) _B+_

Management of session (chairing, moving on, concluding, time-keeping) _A_

Involvement of workshop participants _A_

Visual aids _Difficult to read at times_ _B+_

Team/pair work _A_

Excellent handling of workshop and chairing of discussions.

Handout (33.3%)

Evidence of reading _A_

Organization (relevance, logical progression, length) _B+_

V. Gd. Need to think a little more about how much people need to fill in – can be time waster + prevents people listening.

General comments

A very well run and thought-provoking workshop. Some interesting overheads used, but feel you could have used the one relating to the hospitality industry more constructively – maybe given copy to members of the group.

3.5   Using Student Guide 5: *Writing Essays*

Like the other guides in the series, *Writing Essays* is designed to support students working on their own: the explanations are short and clear, examples are drawn from a wide range of subjects and the activities have full feedback. This guide differs from others in the series, however, in that it develops a particular, highly structured and methodical approach to the processes involved in writing an essay. The approach stems from the conviction that essay writing is a skill, not a talent, and that by breaking the components of the task into bite-sized chunks the skill can be readily learnt.

Advice on essay writing given to students in many course guides works well for those who already have a fair degree of competence. Students who are having difficulties, however, often do not know how to interpret the advice: how do you *plan*? How long should a paragraph be? How do you *develop an idea*? What goes in the conclusion? For these students this guide is saying, 'Try doing it this way'.

The usefulness of the guide to students will increase hugely if you take the time to work through some of the exercises to see how the structured approach developed here would work in your subject, and how you might adapt it, substituting material of your own. Below is a more detailed outline of

- sections you may wish to highlight to students working on their own

- activities that would work particularly well with groups of students, or as part of your overall input to the whole group.

3.5A   Ask key questions (2.1)

You can ask students to use the same approach to clarifying the task as in Section 3.2A above – or the other guides. It can be helpful to subject an essay-writing task to the same scrutiny and analysis as other tasks, if only to counteract the tendency to think that the form of an essay is self-explanatory where other forms require definition.

3.5B   Looking at assessment criteria (2.2/3)

Writing Essays includes three examples of assessment criteria, to demonstrate again how variable the essay form can be. The activity (2.2) is better undertaken in pairs or groups of students than individually. You can add a fourth example of criteria and use the exercise

- to identify criteria for essay writing common to a range of disciplines

- to identify criteria/characteristics specific to the discipline

- as the basis for an exercise for students in generating their own criteria – which you may then wish to use.

You may wish to link this with the section 'Using feedback' (6.1).

3.5C   What is the question asking? (3.1)

This section is the lead-in to a tightly structured chapter on analysing the question and planning an answer. A simple parallel activity is to present two questions on the same topic from past exam papers in your subject, to show how each requires different treatment in the answer.

3.5D   How to analyse the question (3.2)

You can use this approach in a number of ways, for example:

1   Students, in groups of four, analyse the question using the form of notation given. The following discussion in the wider group will demonstrate good analysis, whatever the differences between the groups in the detail of their notation.

2   Run the exercise from the front, using overheads of

- the five-step plan

- the essay titles (one on each OHT)

to allow space for the 'instant plan' (see Section 3.5E below). Move swiftly to a sketched outline plan.

3.5E   How to plan an outline answer (3.3)

You may be greeted with a fair measure of disbelief at the thought of a two-minute essay plan, but this does offer a simple structure for brainstorming. The titles on public policy have been chosen because most people can hazard a guess at the major topic areas, so you can use the subject with students drawn from a range of backgrounds. It can also be helpful in getting students to see structures in writing to use topics outside their particular subject – you can focus on structures unencumbered by knowledge! If you are going to devote a significant amount of time to this, however, you may wish to use questions directly relevant to your students. See sections 3.5I and K below for blueprints you might use.

3.5F   Types of question and styles of answer (3.4)

The division of questions into 'factual' and 'judgement' may seem simplistic. It is, but the text makes clear that the distinction is used as an analytical tool for gaining an understanding of the style and structure of the essay. Chapter 5 (5.5, 5.6) deals with the relationship between points and illustration and argument and evidence. You may wish to touch on the place of personal and academic views at this point, or to acknowledge the issue and return to it later. It is probably better at this stage to treat this as an exercise, and not get too bogged down in detail.

3.5G   A closer look at judgement essays (3.5)

Activity 1: Defining

Most study skills texts have definitions of instructions, and defining them is a useful (brief) group activity. The implications for the style and structure of the essay is the key issue. Williams (1989: pp. 192–8) has a detailed glossary of terms, with examples illustrating their use.

Activity 2: Making judgements

This is a quick, entertaining and instructive exercise, better done with groups of students. Ask each person to draw a line as illustrated for each question, and to mark on their responses as you read out the questions – making substitutions if you want. Ask students to compare their answers with those of their neighbours, or with a wider group. The point is to demonstrate

- how people really do have a very wide range of views, and judgement essays ask you to draw on this

- the relationship between knowledge, interpretation and views.

A quick line-up (see below) helps to show this to the group in an enjoyable and memorable way.

3.5H   A line-up

Pick your controversial question; pick your classroom wall. Mark the point that represents 'Yes, totally, 100%', and the point at the far end of the wall that represents 'No, not at all, 0%', or whatever wording is appropriate to your question. Ask students to get out of their chairs and stand at the place on the wall that they think best represents their views on the issue:

Yes,
totally,
100%

No,
not at all,
0%

Students will have to talk to the people on either side of them to work out if they are in the right place, which should generate lively discussion. You may wish to introduce variants – like a ban on the extremes and the mid-point, the 'I don't know' position – or change the wording to prompt a reshuffle.

3.5l   Blueprint 1: a plan for a judgement essay (3.6)

To the summary of the approach proposed in this section, you might wish to add a simple blank blueprint, shown below, as the basis for a classroom exercise. Material for use with the essay question here is also employed to illustrate the processes of research and the practicalities of reporting, referencing and quoting in 1: EWS, 9: Was Malthus right about population?

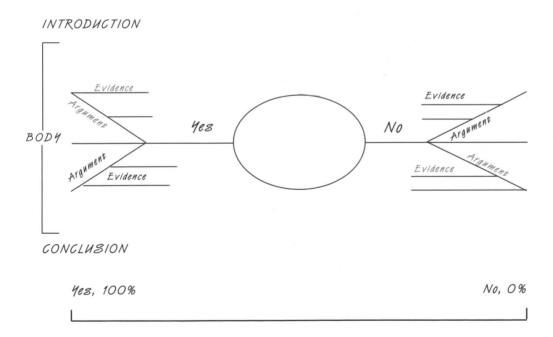

The exercise might run like this:

- distribute the blank blueprint sheets (A4 size)

- ask students to note key arguments and indicative evidence in support both for and against, on the branches shown

- arrange to circulate the sheets, perhaps by sticking them to the wall over a tea break

- have a brief discussion of which points might develop into sections, which might combine, which might be argued both ways, and so on.

3.5J   A closer look at factual essays (3.7)

The two activities here take you right into the structure of the essay.

Activity 1: Defining

This is, as in Section 3.5G above, a useful point of departure.

Activity 2: Following instructions

This activity proposes a variety of outlines to reflect the range of factual essay structures. Undoubtedly, 'factual' essays are harder to organize, not only because people tend to think of them as easier, but also because the variety of instructions is much greater.

3.5K   Blueprint 2: a plan for a factual essay (3.8)

You may wish to run an exercise, as in Blueprint 1 (see Section 3.5I above), based on the blank blueprint below. The blueprint in the Student Guide is based on the essay question *'What are the reasons for. . .'*.

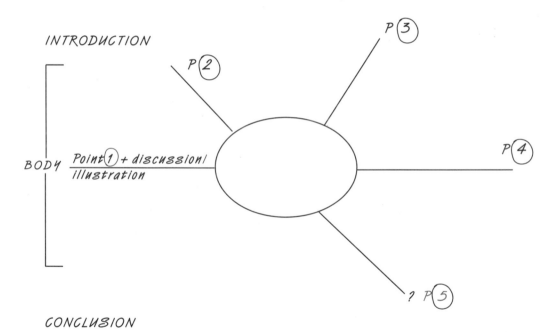

You are more likely to have to adapt the blueprint to meet the requirements of any factual essay you set. You may be able to adapt one of the outlines sketched in the text.

3.5L   Glimpsing the process (Ch. 4)

This chapter is designed to support students in the process of generating material for the essay. It includes brief 'study skills' advice on

- time and process planning (4.2)
- reading strategies (4.3)
- recording sources (4.3); See also 1: EWS, 9
- organizing material (4.4)
- detailed essay planning (4.5)
- drafting (4.6)

- reviewing and editing (4.7)

- the final draft (4.8)

- writing exam essays (4.9); see below.

3.5M Writing exam essays (4.9)

This seems to be a neglected area in the literature on essay-writing techniques, and one students need to rehearse. There are still comparatively few courses that run on 100 per cent coursework, so exams account for a significant proportion of students' final marks. The approach here is clinical and pragmatic: work out

- an overall time budget

- a mark-per-minute budget

- a time-within-question budget

and try it out on a range of sample papers, to which you may wish to add extracts from past papers in your subject. The results of these simple calculations never fail to cause wonderment. The exercise 'Examination Arithmetic' (Williams, 1989: p. 177) provides additional compelling reasons for developing a clear strategy on the use of time in an exam.

3.5N The shape of an essay (5.1)

The point of the images given here is to illustrate

- the coherence of an essay

- the progression of an essay from start to finish

- the linking between sections

and to introduce the visual guide to the chapter ('crunch points'). You may wish to develop the analogies briefly: what is the difference between the beginning of the state/process illustrated and the end? And, of course, to link this with the notion of an essay structure to answer the question.

3.5O Writing introductions (5.2)

The exercise using the material here works well as it stands (you will recognize no. 4 as the extract used at the beginning of this manual). You can run it more than once, substituting extracts from students' essays in your subject. To get the most out of the exercise, allow about an hour. Run the exercise as follows:

1   Ask the students to read the material and mark it individually, using the marking system current in your course/institution. No consultation. (10 minutes)

2   Form pairs, and discuss grades and reasons. (5–10 minutes)

3   Pairs join to form groups of four, with the brief to reach agreement within the group on the grade awarded. They will need to thrash out differences of opinion, and be prepared to justify the grade they award to the whole group. (10–15 minutes)

4   Ask each group of four to feed back to the whole group their verdicts on the extracts, one at a time. Make sure they give reasons and cite evidence. Allow time for discussion. (20 minutes)

5   Extract general points and advice about how to write an introduction. You could also ask groups to rewrite one extract to make it as near perfect as possible.

By the end of this plenary session, anything you ever wanted to say about the characteristics of good, bad and indifferent pieces of work is likely to have been covered.

If there is a problem, it is usually that the students are too harsh in their judgement. While individual students may start off with an eccentric view of the merits of a piece of writing, the consensus is invariably spot on. This sequence can be adapted for any exercise involving a critical evaluation of model material (see Section 2.5 above).

3.5P   Writing paragraphs (5.3)

A simple blueprint for how to write a paragraph is given here. It differs from the general run of advice on how to write a paragraph in the stress laid on the need to conclude – to show the link with the topic sentence, the next paragraph and the section heading or title.

Activity 1 is resourced in the text (identify the structure of a paragraph); Activity 2 is a guided exercise in free writing. These activities are more likely to be relevant to specific groups of students with identified difficulties in writing, such as international students and mature and alternative entry students. For additional material, see also 1: EWS, 7.

3.5Q   Building an argument (5.4)

This section takes the form of an extended activity. It is tightly structured and fully resourced to make it suitable for students working on their own. If a student needs this kind of work, the tutor should make the specific suggestion. It can also be used for supportive work with individual students and special interest groups, as in section 3.5P above.

An extension of the activity is to consider other pieces of writing against the 'template' of the five questions and sketches: what is the argument? How is the argument built? etc.

3.5R   Using evidence (5.5)

This brief section only touches on this crucial area in academic writing. The need to support argument with evidence, points with illustration, is presented as an aspect of courtesy to the reader, and provides a point of departure for work within individual disciplines.

3.5S   Using other people's ideas (5.6)

Again, this section views the need to cite, refer and quote accurately from the perspective of the reader: to empower the reader to challenge, agree with, research further the issues in question. This approach is designed to go some way towards counteracting the nonchalance demonstrated by many students in relation to the need to cite references accurately and fully. Simple models of references are given. See 1: EWS, 9, for a fuller look at these issues.

3.5T   Writing conclusions (5.7)

The conclusion is perhaps the most problematic aspect of students' essay writing, more so even than the introduction.

There are two elements to the exercise.

1   Run this exercise as in section 3.5O above, following the same sequence and approximate timing.

2   Ask students to grade the essay as whole, based on their reading of the introductions and conclusions only. This will lead to a discussion of how impressions are formed, confirmed or counteracted, and touch on aspects of presentation ('I can't read it, so I'll fail it'!). What messages do they take away from the exercise?

As with the exercise on introductions, you can repeat it using material from your field.

3.5U   Self- and peer assessment (5.10)

This section provides students with some prompts as to why you might ask them for self- or peer assessment. You may wish to draw on some of the approaches outlined in Section 2.8 above.

3.5V   Other forms of writing (6.1)

This section places the move towards setting tasks to be presented in a wider range of written formats in the context of the audience for whom the piece is to be written and the purpose it is intended to fulfil. The forms outlined in the text are

- portfolio

- 300-word essay

- article

- poster

- creative writing of various sorts.

Examples of some of these are illustrated below.

i)   Creative writing

The forms creative writing can take are virtually limitless. Below are a couple of tasters:

A pamphlet: The state of our cities (1856)

Reader, our nation a mere five years ago presented itself as the workshop of the world. The Chrystal Palace was a glittering display of achievement in manufacturers of all kinds. It has made some men rich. But do not forget that our national wealth has a human cost. Our working men, our working women and children live in conditions often unfit for the lowest kind of civilization. They work long hours in dirty, noisy and dangerous factories where mortality and death are daily attendant . . .

A letter: The effect of pesticides

Country Landowners Association Gazette

Monday 25th January

Dear Sir, in response to the letter written by Major John Thomas, published on Tuesday 14th January, I feel I must exercise my 'Right to Reply'.

Between 1945 and 1985, estimates suggest that 40% of the remaining broad leaved woodlands, 20% of the hedgerows and 25% of the sem... environments (w... moors) 'dis...

pesticide residues. A survey in 1985 on pesticides currently being used in Britain suggested that 49 were possible carcinogens, 61 may cause defects and 90 possible allergens.

Fertiliser... c...

ii) Portfolio

Below is an extract from the module handbook in which the students' task in compiling an individual portfolio is outlined. (See also Section 1.3 above.)

<u>Individual Portfolio (15%)</u>

As the module progresses you will be learning about managing people through a variety of methods. You will be carrying out workshop tasks, researching topics, presenting information, talking to people and so on. All through the module we would like you to collect evidence of your learning based on your experiences and activities and your reflections about these experiences in relation to the concepts and ideas that underpin the module. The assessment criteria for the portfolio are based on Honey and Mumford's (1986) version of the learning cycle:

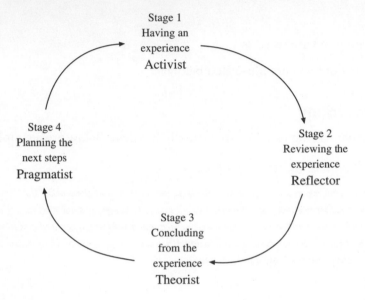

Source: Honey and Mumford, 1986

The Learning Cycle

As they explain, although learning can start anywhere on the cycle, no one stage of the cycle is effective on its own as a learning procedure. Your portfolio will be assessed according to how far you have achieved the following:

1   demonstrated that you have carried out workshop activities, intelligence gathering, working in a group, etc.

2   shown that you have reflected on your experiences and drawn out learning points

3   related your experiences to concepts and ideas covered in lectures, books, articles and workshops

4   put forward recommendations/proposals to solve problems, develop approaches, etc., which derive from 1–3.

It is up to you to decide what is put into the portfolio and how to present it. Ideas for content include evidence from workshop tasks such as completed person specifications, feedback sheets about your performance in role plays, self-evaluation or peer evaluation sheets, or your reflections about any of the tasks you have been asked to carry out. Try to make the presentation creative and interesting for the reader.

(from Module Handbook Management of Human Resources in the Hospitality Industry, reproduced with thanks to Liz Price, Oxford Brookes University)

Some excellent work has been produced in response to this task:

Introduction

This portfolio aims to demonstrate what the author has gained from Module 3173. It contains a number of different kinds of entry, from 'diary style' reflections on lecture points and workshop exercises, to breakdowns of seminar presentations. It does, however, continually reflect a personal way of thinking, and hence does not contain re-written lecture notes or workshop handouts. The way it has been compiled (week by week) loosely ties to Honey and Mumford's (1986) Learning Cycle – the activist stage relating to the author attending lectures and workshops. From there, activities were mulled over and reviewed, and ideas written down in this portfolio (theorist stage). Finally conclusions drawn from the experience demonstrate the pragmatist stage, and the cycle starts again.

Week 1

Lecture

1 Unitary v Pluralist frames of reference

A new concept for me, and one which I'm not 100% convinced by. A unitary approach seems more likely in smaller (family run?) organizations, and wouldn't work in larger units . . .

2 Personnel v Human Resource Management

Personnel management more appropriate for manufacturing industries of the early 20th century. HRM has more contemporary relevance . . .

Workshop

1 Groupwork

Formed base groups. Fortunately I'm with my house mates Claire and Vic, with whom I get on pretty well – they'd probably disagree. Identified pros and cons of working in groups. Initial thoughts were that the exercise was a waste of time . . . might not be the case if I was working with two complete strangers. It was concluded that the 'free-loader' problem could be resolved by various methods (identifying common interests, injecting humour etc.). I cannot relate to this! Past experience shows that if you get stuck with a lazy sod, nothing you can do changes the situation . . . these people do not care how well they do. If you want the work done properly, you do it yourself, and avoid raised blood pressure and heart tremors.

Week 2

Preparation for interview exercise next week. It becomes apparent just how much preparation is needed for an interview to be effective (from the interviewer's point of view). A pre-prepared set of questions or question guidelines seems essential, as well as a good knowledge of the candidate. Initial fears of 'cringe factor' of such an exercise, it may become too ridiculous / embarrassing to have any worth . . . we will see.

Week 3

Interview exercise

Despite all fears last week of this exercise being rather a waste of time, it was in fact extremely useful, and even quite fun. The preparation our base group did before the exercise was shown to have been vital – the interviews would have been ineffective if we hadn't briefed ourselves fully on the candidates, and the vacancy we were recruiting for. Initial nervousness was soon forgotten, and the situation became more relaxed and informal.

Learning outcomes

i) A well structured interview is effective – greeting, introduction, explanation of proceedings, interview, closing. This requires a fair degree of preparation by the interviewer, and perhaps a written checklist to refer to.

ii) In the same way, the interviewee must be fully prepared – my first one was, and hence came across very well . . . However, it was obvious once or twice that she was reciting a pre-prepared script, and this surely must be avoided – as the interviewer, I found this easy to spot . . .

iii) A good interview is rather like a relaxed conversation, instead of a question and answer session. This facilitates both parties to communicate the required information effectively.

iv) The exercise was particularly useful for me, as I had a job interview myself that afternoon . . .

Reproduced with thanks to Dan Shotton, Hotel and Catering Management student

iii) Poster

The evolution of a task

This section shows how a writing task set on a particular topic on the syllabus of an engineering module changed over time. The task was to engage the students in a consideration of the impact of political, economic, social and technical factors on the construction industry. The form the task took changed from an essay, to an assignment or case study, to a poster.

As an essay

The task was to write an essay along these lines:

```
Outline the strategies used by construction firms in response
to political, economic and technical factors beyond their
control. Evaluate the effectiveness of these strategies.
```

As an assignment or case study

The brief for the task in this form included the following:

In this assignment you should take responsibility for gathering materials and presenting ideas and arguments on a topic which you choose . . . Identify a problem of special interest to you, and involving the interface between civil engineering or building and the natural, economic, social or political world . . . Build up a file of material related to the problem, including such things as newspaper cuttings, magazine articles, comments from other people and notes made from books or reports relevant to the subject. But, above all, include your own thoughts and analysis (recognizing that they may change over time). At the end of the file should be your analysis of the problem, the surrounding circumstances and proposed or attempted solutions, and your own conclusions . . .

As a poster or wallchart

An extract from the brief for the task in the form of a poster or wallchart is shown below. There follows a wallchart produced by one student and examples of feedback on the assignment from the tutor.

Coursework No. 2: worth 25% of module coursework

Hand back   lecture on Friday in
Week 3

Background

Those managing programmes of construction work as clients (e.g., the Department of Transport, port and airport authorities or major commercial or industrial enterprises) or managing construction companies or firms of consultants need constantly to adapt to changing circumstances external to any project or firms specific issues and over which they have no control. These are referred to as the PEST factors. PEST stands for Political, Economic, Social and Technical . . .

Task

Produce an A3 sized wall-chart identifying classifying and illustrating the PEST factors. The chart may use lines or arrows to show logical connections or consequences, sketches and should included information or examples possibly in boxes of text. Browse through back numbers (go several years back) of New Civil Engineering, Building, New Builder or other construction industry periodical and use at least five "snippets" of information (e.g., in the blocks of text) from articles found in the periodicals . . .

For a high mark the chart should briefly indicate the strategies used by managements of construction firms in response to the kinds of problems they face. For example most firms keep capital expenditure to a minimum since workload is inevitably unstable (why?) (but how is capital expenditure kept to a minimum?).

No folders please: fold your sheet to A4 size and staple a cover sheet and sheet of reference and bibliography details and this sheet. Use a standard convention for referencing, which should provide full details so that someone else could go straight to the relevant page.

Objectives

1   To help you to see construction management in context.

2   To help you to appreciate the diversity of technical, legal and other problems dealt with by civil engineers and builders.

3   To help you to identify problems specific to the construction industry.

P.E.S.T. FACTORS AFFECTING CIVIL ENGINEERING PROJECTS

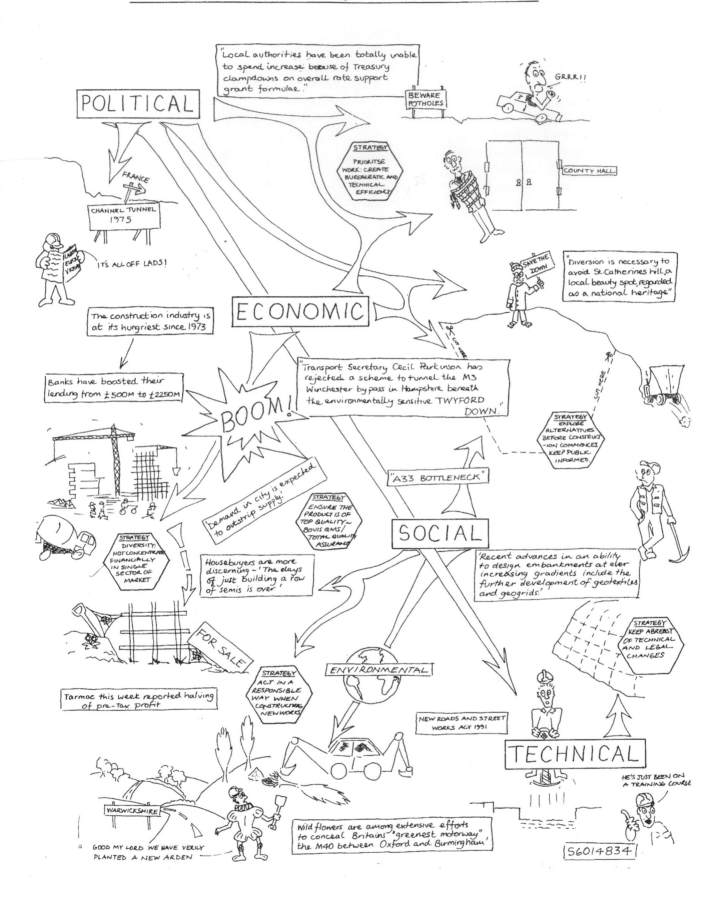

MODULE 4452
CONSTRUCTION PLANNING AND MANAGEMENT

General comment on wallchart coursework

Assessing this proved much more rewarding than assessing essays. I think everybody benefited from doing the task in that they had to think and learn about the reality of construction management in a turbulent environment where the best-laid plans usually have to be revised. It was also a chance to explore skills of presentation using graphical techniques as well as words. This was the first time that this type of coursework has been used in this subject and the specification was possibly more vague than some would have liked. Nevertheless there were many excellent pieces of work and most people obviously worked out what was needed. Many people took advantage of the medium to produce imaginative, attractive and informative submissions. Others merely used cuttings to show a few examples of the PEST (or STEP) factors without much attention to classifying the various types of causes and their impact on the construction industry. One or two people interpreted 'wall-chart' as 'collage', which is an art-form primarily intended for visual impact rather than a means of conveying information and analysis. Good wall-charts are better than essays at conveying thinking and a quick 'wall-chart' type diagram is probably the best form of preparing notes for an essay.

Assessment Criteria (hand in with your essay)

Self-assessment. Please ring the appropriate letter –

(e) excellent, (g) good, (a) average, (f) fair, (p) poor

1 Is there sufficient detail?   (e) g a f p

2 Is there a clear and logical structure to the chart with sensible grouping and sub-grouping?   e (g) a f p

3 Is the chart attractive and does it convey information clearly and effectively?   (e) g a f p

4 Are the issues or points shown relevant   e (g) a f p

5 Are there sufficient examples, clarification, explanation and evidence?   e g (a) f p

6 Is there evidence of research, particularly in the form of facts, figures and references (full).   e (g) a f p   *Cannot identify source of each cutting.*

Overall an entertaining and informative presentation with evidence of much creative thought.

(Extracts reproduced with thanks to Nick Spencer-Chapman and students)

Further reading

Brookes, A. and Grundy, P. (1990). *Writing for Study Purposes*. Cambridge: CUP.

Brown, S., Rust, C. and Gibbs, G. (1994). *Strategies for Diversifying Assessment*. Oxford: Oxford Centre for Staff Development.

Gibbs, G., Habeshaw, S. and Habeshaw, T. (1989). *53 Interesting Ways of Helping your Students to Study Effectively*. 2nd edn, Bristol: Technical and Educational Services.

Habeshaw, S. and Steeds, D. (1987). *53 Interesting Communications Exercises for Science Students*. Bristol: Technical and Educational Services.

Trzeciak, J. and Mackay S. (1994). *Study Skills for Academic Writing*. Hemel Hempstead: Prentice-Hall.

Williams, K. (1989). *Study Skills*. London: Macmillan.